Musical Composition

Reginald Smith Brindle

Musical
Composition

Oxford   New York
Oxford University Press
1986

Oxford University Press, Walton Street, Oxford OX2 6DP

Oxford New York Toronto
Delhi Bombay Calcutta Madras Karachi
Petaling Jaya Singapore Hong Kong Tokyo
Nairobi Dar es Salaam Cape Town
Melbourne Auckland

and associated companies in
Beirut Berlin Ibadan Nicosia

OXFORD is a trade mark of Oxford University Press

British Library Cataloguing in Publication Data
Brindle, Reginald Smith
    Musical composition.
    1. Composition (Music)
    I. Title
    781.6'1   MT40

    ISBN 0-19-317108-2
    ISBN 0-19-317107-4 Pbk

Library of Congress Cataloging in Publication Data
    Brindle, Reginald Smith, 1917–
    Musical composition.
    Includes index.
    1. Composition (Music)   I. Title.
    MT40.B89 1986   781.6'1   85-15369
    ISBN 0-19-317108-2
    ISBN 0-19-317107-4 (pbk.)

iv

Contents

Acknowledgements

Copyright music examples in this book are quoted by kind permission of the following publishers.

Boosey & Hawkes Music Publishers Ltd: Benjamin Britten, *Peter Grimes* © Copyright 1945 by Boosey & Hawkes Music Publishers Ltd, *Seven Sonnets of Michelangelo* © Copyright 1943 by Boosey & Co Ltd, *War Requiem* © Copyright 1962 by Boosey & Hawkes Music Publishers Ltd; Gerald Finzi, *My spirit sang all day* © Copyright 1937 by Oxford University Press. Copyright assigned 1969 to Boosey & Hawkes Music Publishers Ltd; Roberto Gerhard, String Quartet No. 1 © Copyright 1958 by Keith Prowse Music Publishers Ltd. Copyright assigned 1979 to Boosey & Hawkes Publishers Ltd for all countries; Igor Stravinsky, *Canticum sacrum* © Copyright 1956 by Hawkes & Son (London) Ltd, *Symphonies of Wind Instruments* © Copyright 1952 by Hawkes & Son (London) Ltd (revised version), *Symphony of Psalms* © Copyright 1948 by Hawkes & Son (London) Ltd (revised version), *Threni* © Copyright 1958 by Boosey & Co Ltd. *Canticum sacrum, Symphony of Psalms, Symphonies of Wind Instruments, Threni* — by Stravinsky, *Peter Grimes, War Requiem, Seven Sonnets of Michelangelo* — by Britten, *My spirit sang all day* — by Finzi, and String Quartet No. 1 — by Gerhard are specifically excluded from any blanket photocopying arrangement. Bruzzichelli: Bruno Bartolozzi, *Serenata*; Sylvano Bussotti, *Siciliano*; Bruno Maderna, Oboe Concerto. Campbell Connelly & Co Ltd: Thomas 'Fats' Waller, 'Honeysuckle Rose'. Chappell & Co, Inc: Thomas 'Fats' Waller, 'Honeysuckle Rose' Copyright © 1929 by Santly Bros, Inc. Copyright renewed, Waller's interest controlled by Chappell & Co, Inc (Intersong Music, Publisher). International copyright secured; all rights reserved. Durand S. A. Editions Musicales, Paris/UMP: Olivier Messiaen, *O sacrum convivium* © 1937. Editions A. Leduc, Paris/UMP: Olivier Messiaen, *Messe de la Pentecôte*. Editions Arima Ltd & Durand S. A. Editions Musicales, Paris/UMP: Maurice Ravel, Sonatine © 1905. Edizioni Suvini Zerboni, Milan: Bruno Bartolozzi, *The Solitary*; Luciano Berio, *Serenata 1*; Luigi Dallapiccola, *Cinque Canti, Il prigioniero, Quaderno musicale di Annalibera*; Franco Donatoni, *Algo*; Goffredo Petrassi, *Nunc*; Henri Pousseur, *Quintette*. EMI Music Publishing Ltd: Harry Akst, 'Dinah' © 1925 Waterson Berlin and Snyder Inc, now Mills Music Inc USA. International Music Publi-

Introduction

I hesitated long before beginning this book. Everybody tells me it is impossible to teach composition, so a book on the subject would seem beyond the bounds of possibility. However, in writing down what I have taught over the last thirty years, I am convinced that if composition is 'not teachable', at least a vast amount of information can be given — so much that one can virtually cover the whole subject. The only great gap is where one would expect — in the areas of subjective choice, aesthetic discrimination, intuition, and invention. Inevitably, these intangible factors cannot be taught, but the rest makes up a very sizeable amount of learning which can be passed on. Even in the subjective areas, there is not a complete void, as the advice and recommendations of my text may prove.

I am convinced that some attempt at composition is a necessary experience for all musicians, for through composition musicians can teach themselves so much about the depths of music, and feel the mystery of our art as they could in no other way. To compose is one of the most wonderful experiences God has given us, and the journey into our imagination is something other mortals may never experience.

However, I must admit to having had failures. Many students have failed to respond, but sometimes there have been unexpected flowerings as dormant talents reacted to new ideas and discoveries.

This book is designed for school-leavers or the first two years of a university course. As a guide, I have usually tried to reach Chapter 9 in the first two terms, spending the third on a study of electronic music. In the second year I complete the book (which means moving quickly), and spend the third working with a chosen few on longer pieces or exercises in the student's preferred idiom. In this way, the subject matter of this book can be covered in two years and thus provides a base for subsequent expansion.

I am well aware that many parts of the book need supplemental reading in various technical disciplines, and also specific historical and analytical studies. Coverage of all these factors would have needed several volumes. In justification for my avoiding the side-paths of many special studies (harmony, counterpoint, orchestration, etc.), I would say that as composition is the unification of many disciplines, one would hardly expect it to be studied on its own, without other adequate preparation. This book therefore aims at gathering the threads of many disciplines and unifying them in the greatest study of all.

1 Composition: key to musicianship

The teaching of composition is a controversial issue. In the music profession (including students) there are two strongly held opinions: one is that composition cannot be taught; the other that composition should not be taught. My own experiences have been rather varied. My Italian composition teachers (Pizzetti and Dallapiccola) were both enigmatic and disappointing, even counterproductive. Where I looked for stimulus, encouragement, and learning, I found none, so inevitably I felt some sense of frustration and discouragement. Yet one can learn from others. Young musicians like Donatoni, Bartolozzi, Nono, Maderna, and Berio gave me plenty of ideas, even if (looking back) they led me up the wrong road.

Personally, I think we are born composers and not made. My most successful work, in terms of sales and gramophone recordings, is a little guitar piece which was written well before I had lessons in the theory of music. It is even possible that I would be where I am today, or even far better off, if I had continued to be self-taught, never taking a single composition lesson. But I doubt it. The advice and guidance of others can be absolutely invaluable. In the ways of art and music, we advance by stepping in each other's footsteps, following a path and then branching off on our own. With a wise guide we can reach our ultimate goal more quickly.

This book is primarily addressed to students who have a lot to learn, who need to be helped over the first hurdles. To those young musicians who already have bulging portfolios of compositions under their arms, who already know by instinct what they want to write and how to do it, I would offer only a little advice: get to know plenty of scores, and find out how the music is made and why, so that you can use the techniques if you wish. The music of others can fill you with ideas, which you can make genuinely your own. If you have a teacher, let him be informative and stimulating − even provoking − but never pedantic, imposing his own will, or critical in a destructive way. The only valid criticism is constructive criticism. If your teacher destroys without reconstructing something worthy, say goodbye to him.

I think this book could also be valuable to students who were not born with an instinctive grasp of 'how to do it', even if they never feel the urge to compose at all. For I believe there are several good reasons why all musicians, whatever their ultimate aim, should undertake a course in composition. First of all, I believe that composition is the synthesis of all other musical disciplines — the ultimate unity, and the keystone. It puts together all the theories or techniques that make up the essence of music, its performance, and its study from a historical point of view. This opinion, that composition is the key discipline in a musical education, is by no means universally held, but over the the last forty years I have seen a constant drift towards this attitude, and there is no doubt that it will continue. Even some enlightened directors of primary school education are insisting that composition, however simple, should begin in early years, and should have priority over listening and playing. For creating demands understanding, whereas hearing and performing require a more superficial knowledge.[1]

Student performers can benefit particularly from composition. They are often the most reluctant to become involved in it, since they need to spend so much time in instrumental practice, but they will never play music really superbly, in spite of all their technique, without inside experience; with it, they will be able to recreate the music just as the composer himself conceived it. A performer should be able to compose well enough to know what is behind the notes, what must be stressed and what subdued, what should be made to sing out and what should be almost concealed, like the scaffolds behind a stage set. For musical notation is still a very imperfect medium of communication. It may give us a lot of information (as is the custom today) or very little more than the notes and their place in time, but it can never give us more than a hint of the emotive message which is the composer's real intention, and which is what music is all about. A performer who has composed will divine this message more clearly than one who has not.

Again, performers may have to improvise. This supreme form of spontaneous composition was once the greatest proof of musicianship. If a lutenist could not conjure up a fantasia or a saltarello at a moment's notice, there was little prospect of him having any supper. An organist had to be able to throw off either a cheerful blast or a solemn dirge in an instant. But in the last century emphasis was placed instead on precise note-reading, the player's own inventive powers being cast aside. Now things have gone full circle, many scores, whether serious or 'pop', leaving a great deal to the player's creative faculties. He has to be able to shine on these occasions, or he will be left out of the next session list. To improvise well, the player must know about melodic phrase construction, formal principles, stylistic dictates, and idiomatic limitations; without this knowledge his efforts could well be meaningless, out of style, even destructive. This is another reason for performers to study composition. Their livelihood may well depend on it.

[1] 'No one who observes education in music can be satisfied with what he observes. The crux lies in a prejudice worded in the Primary Memorandum as follows: "The child begins by listening". Hence, sensory experience is given priority over motor-experience: listening comes before playing; the reading of music before the writing of music: and all our errors and defeats follow ineluctably.' (Notes on *The Perceptual/Motor Match*, summing up Newell C. Kephart's theories, issued by the Scottish Education Department.)

Even if one is only a 'listener' or a 'reader' — and some distinguished musicians such as critics and musicologists may limit their activity to looking at scores or listening to performances — the study of composition is valuable. It gives a greater insight into the processes which created the music, the priority of certain elements, their degree of originality (or mediocrity), and so on. Additionally, if critics have themselves experienced the weight of labour in composition, the degree of self-criticism needed, even only the tiresomeness of copying scores and parts, they may perhaps be more benign in their criticisms. Perhaps they may even remember that music criticism should not be merely destructive, but should be aimed instead at illumination, at preparing the listener to receive the music's emotive message. Especially in the case of modern music, this can be a most challenging task — far greater than the easy dismissal of music which may be obscure and even enigmatic, yet which has a profound humanity in its heart.

Composition is both an intellectual discipline and a creative stimulus. Chess is an excellent intellectual discipline, but it only stretches the mind. Composition, whether it stretches the mind or not, takes us on that crucial journey into our own imagination which is one of man's greatest experiences. To think is at least something, but to think creatively is to live a satisfying and absorbing intellectual life, one which can be enjoyed only by a chosen few.

Finally, let me quote what I believe to be the greatest proverb in the field of learning, and which is particularly apt in music: 'I hear and I forget; I see and I remember; I do and I *understand*'. This is the point of my book. If all musicians were to 'do', to compose, think out a few notes, however rudimentary, they would understand. They would have a lesson about their trade which no other teaching can give.

2 First ideas

Nothing empties the mind more quickly than a sheet of blank manuscript paper — especially if we have no clear idea of what we want to write. To make blank paper a less daunting sight I like to cover the top with scribblings in strong black ink — just fragments of melody, chords, anything. I find that ideas, perhaps generated by the scribblings, then begin to flow, so that after crossing out unwanted jottings I can carry on with relative ease. In short, if we can only get the mind moving, undeterred by the blank page, it will keep on. Work creates work, and a mind which has begun to generate ideas will be impatient to move forward.

If we cannot make a start, or if we come to a stop all too soon, it is because we still have no vision of what we want to create. At one time I expected inspiration to come down like a bolt from the blue, but found that when it came it was only a brief fragment which dug its heels in and resisted any attempt to make it go forward. Or I used to wake in the night with what seemed a revelation and would copy it down there and then, only to find that in the morning it would seem mediocre and worthy only to be thrown away, perhaps in a fit of bad temper.

Though this first period of frustration can be upsetting, it can largely be avoided if we rely not on inspirational visitations but on some fairly concrete decisions. We must decide what kind of music we want to write, and for what instruments; how many movements we want, and in what forms. Then, how does the beginning fit into the form of the first movement, and precisely what kind of material should it be — simply introductory, or atmospheric, or setting out the main thematic material of the movement? Gradually, an accurate plan of what is going to happen is formed, and perhaps we may be able to say: 'This is going to be a string quartet, which will begin with a solo cello giving out a theme which will become the basic material for the entire work, which will be in one movement. The music will start slowly with long and sweeping melodic phrases capable of emotive development. After the cello has played the main material, this will be taken up by the viola, then the violins, in a contrapuntal texture which will then give way to a full statement of the theme, strongly, in unison.' We then have to get down to just what this cello theme is going to be, the form, the phrase formations, what key to use, what note to start on, the rhythmic shape of the first bars, and so on.

Having decided what to do, we are presented with a quite precise and well-defined problem, which may often be solved by sheer skill and technical craftsmanship, even if the result is not ideal and needs to be improved on later. The important thing is to get started. The perfect solution may present itself only at an unexpected moment — perhaps while we are waiting at the traffic lights. The mind works all the time; we can't stop it.

Of course, I have missed out, for the sake of simplification, some factors of paramount importance. The basic character of the music must be uniform throughout. To avoid an impression of inconsistency — even oddness at times — music must be formed from the same kind of material from beginning to end. The musical language must be kept within precise confines, and it is well for us to have a precise knowledge of the basic materials we use. Is the harmony diatonic, chromatic, tonal, or non-tonal? Of what elements is it comprised? Is the melody kept within a conventional field, or do we have personal idiosyncracies which give it a special character? In other words, we must know and remain faithful to our own musical language. In any case, to know the exact 'building blocks' of our trade is a great time-saver. How often have I shown students exactly what language they have unconsciously used, sometimes wasting hours fumbling at the keyboard, trying to find the right notes? On the other hand, it is perhaps prudent not to show students too hastily how they have wasted their time and effort. I remember one student was most annoyed with me when I showed him (rather too quickly) how he could have written his music more easily if he had begun with the knowledge that he was using only the six notes of a whole-tone scale.

Another important factor must be borne in mind when we begin a piece: too much detail at that stage can be a handicap. If the music is melodic, we must think only of melody and get a good part of a theme on paper before we begin to think of the harmony which should go with it. Too early a concentration on the harmony can obstruct the melodic flow. In fact, the whole melody may be complete before we turn back to concentrate on harmony, which in all probability may be suggested by the melody itself. How many students have come to me with only two bars of music — melody and harmony all complete — and said they couldn't go any further. Of course they couldn't, having concentrated on too much at once, without regard for what was to follow.

The same is true of music which begins in other ways — with only harmonies or textures. Make sure the music flows forwards before turning back to fill in the details. The movement of the top or bottom part is often enough to serve as a guide for all the rest of the music. (Note how the magic chord sequence which begins and echoes throughout Dvořák's *Largo* from the 'New World' Symphony has a top part which really has its own sense of direction. In spite of aiming at harmonic progression as a prime target, Dvořák must have written the contour of the upper part first.)

Even after we have finished a piece, it is worth looking back and reconsidering the beginning, which is after all the most important moment of all. Perhaps we can now improve it, or, with the advantage of being able to see the movement as a whole, decide a special introduction is needed, possibly using some material which occurs later on. Perhaps we can link it in some way with the ending, making a rational formal design. In others words, our 'first ideas' may not always be our best ones. They can be improved, cut into better shape, polished, transplanted, or even discarded once the complete work is set out before us.

It is also worth saying a word about writing at the piano. Students sometimes think this is 'prohibited', but this is nonsense — to play what we write is excellent, for it teaches us to associate notation with sound results, and playing at the keyboard may also stimulate creative ideas. However, it is good to think, to imagine, before playing, as a guard against following to excess the automatism of our fingers, which have learned to play certain patterns and will tend to reproduce them without regard for the new composition if rational control is not kept vigilant. I used to write at a table with my back to the piano, so that I could check what I had written when necessary and at the same time discover the sound of what was already on paper. One day I realized I hadn't used the piano for months, that I no longer needed it to convey the sound of what I had written. So, by all means use the piano, but let it not be a substitute for rational thought.

3 Formal principles

We could discuss musical form at considerable length, and even write a treatise on that subject alone. But here I prefer only to draw attention to those basic principles which underlie all matters of form, whether in short phrases, large movements, or even gigantic symphonies, leaving aside the study of conventional forms (sonata form, binary form, etc.) which the student can find better illustrated elsewhere. Here we are concerned with the basic principles, on which all else depends and which may eventually be applied to longer movements as well as to short sections.

Before we begin, however, I would like to point out that a great deal of contemporary music has been written which belies much or all of what I have to say. This kind of music, of which I contributed my own part, deliberately aimed at beginning anew, ignoring the conventions of the past; the only universal ideal was that the new music should be completely unlike whatever was heard before. Within that every composer tried to be different, mistaking novelty for originality and quality. Naturally enough, a confused situation arose, during which old conventions such as melody and harmony were jettisoned. The success or failure of this operation is certainly not under discussion here, my reason for bringing it in being simply to point out that music, even good music, can be written which does not abide by standard formal principles. However, I would say that any branch of art − be it music, painting, sculpture, literature, drama, or poetry − which abandons formal principles to the point of formlessness is doomed to failure: form allows a sense of completeness in a work of art, one that can be grasped by us and held in our memories. The fact that much modern art is quite unmemorable − and modern music particularly so − is perhaps a result of formal weakness, and is certainly the reason for its perishable quality. So though these remarks are addressed to beginners, I believe that some of the formal ideas could well be considered anew by the great number of talented young composers who are either clambering up the rungs of the ladder of fame or jostling for a foothold.

Why, then, is form so important? Certainly, it was at one time essential for certain musical movements to be of a precise length, for otherwise the dancers of gavottes and minuets would find themselves in sorry confusion. But precise length is purely a secondary issue in art music. The real importance of musical form is of a psychological nature: music is an emotive message; and good form ensures that the message is convincing, unified, and complete. Nothing should be allowed to disturb the emotional flow, nor should the interest be given the chance to lapse. Between our sense of beginning and of concluding we should be led on a journey which is not only logical but is also of continuous emotional interest.

Of course, this is an enormous generalization. Some musical forms (especially canon and fugue) have an element of intellectual appeal which dictates the form to a considerable degree. Other music, especially from the Orient, can be almost eventless, so that the emotions are lulled into a state of passive acceptance. And yet other music, especially in opera, may have abrupt, rapid changes which are deliberately designed to throw our emotions into turmoil. There is indeed quite an amount of contemporary music which seems designed to keep us in a state of perpetual shock. But here we cannot consider what is abnormal, we must confine our study of formal principles to what is to be found in most Western music.

One of the greatest problems in form, in fact the cardinal problem, is that of achieving unity. Now unity can be guaranteed simply by using the same material from beginning to end, as is done as a matter of course in many fugues. But how dull a poorly constructed fugue can be. If we listen to music which continues for too long without change the mind tends to go to sleep, and at best listening becomes an effort, so that in spite of our concentration other thoughts tend to slip in. But if the music changes, our attention is immediately alerted, and we listen to the new message with pleasure. Similarly this 'new message' cannot be allowed to go on for too long, as the mind will require yet another change. It is here that we must take care. For though the factor of change is essential to retain interest, it is the thing most guaranteed to destroy unity. Continuous change makes it impossible to remember what has gone before, or to relate one part to another. Inevitably, the absence of a sense of completeness or fulfilment leaves us dissatisfied and forgetful of what we have heard.

What is the solution to these problems of unity and sustaining interest? I think it can best be found by looking at the visual arts, and having myself once been an architect I would like to use an architectural illustration. Let us go for a moment to the Acropolis at Athens, a well-spread group of different buildings, all of the fifth century BC. Let us say that we have gone to see the Parthenon in particular, reputedly the greatest building ever conceived by man. We stand for some time looking at its forty-six Doric columns (some of them, sadly, fallen), appreciating the entasis, the capital formation, the details of the entablature, and so on. But inevitably, at a certain point, we turn to look at the Erechtheion, some way off. Our eyes and minds have felt the need for change, not only a change of view but also the psychological relief and stimulus of thinking of something new. Fortunately, though the Erechtheion is quite different, it is not too different to break our mood. We view it with pleasure for some time, and then, inevitably, at the right psychological moment, we turn back to the Parthenon with our interest renewed, perhaps moving to a different viewpoint, to see things differently. Then, again inevitably, we turn away for another change of view, perhaps this time towards the Propylaea and Nike Apteros. These again suit our mood, but at the last we turn for a final lingering view of the Parthenon, reflecting perhaps on the ultimate destiny of the material works of man. Our interest is satiated, and we are pleased to have seen not only the Parthenon but other great buildings as well. And though the objects of our gaze have been varied, the experience has been a unified one, for they were the result of one artistic mood, erected within a few years almost 2,500 years ago.

Now music is like this. It is a journey in time, which we begin with an experience which completely absorbs our attention but which, at a certain psychological point, demands change. At this point, new but emotionally-related material should appear to capture our interest, and itself give way to what we heard first, which we greet with renewed interest. This process can continue, turning aside and turning back, and as long as the emotive flow is not disrupted unity is preserved, while our interest is constantly kept alive and rewarded.

This principle of renewing interest while preserving unity is the basis of all successful conventional musical forms. The alternation of something familiar and something new, of 'statement and change', can be used in many ways, to build small paragraphs, longer sections, or lengthy movements.

One of the most obvious examples of this principle of 'statement and change' is the old *concerto grosso* form, where the main orchestra, or 'tutti', always plays the same musical substance, each statement being separated by the solo 'concertino' group playing something different, usually of a virtuoso character. This is a very pleasant form, easy to grasp, and is obviously already very close to the later rondo form. Here, between a number of statements of the same theme or section, contrasting sections are introduced, which may or may not appear again. This can result in a number of different formal patterns, such as ABACADA, or ABACABA, where A represents the recurring material and B, C, and D periods of change. Such alternations of musical sections are of course the basis of most conventional musical forms (except those based on a single theme, such as fugue), and this important principle, of statement and change, coupled with the use of repetition, forms my main point. However, every piece of music is different and has its own problems, and it is therefore necessary to point out a few pitfalls, and to make a few special recommendations.

Repetition is something many students avoid at all costs, and in their early music they tend not to repeat a single bar in an entire composition. I have often shown them how using repetition wisely, they could have halved their labour and produced a more coherent work. In fact, the degree of repetition we can tolerate seems to depend on the special ability of a composer. Beethoven may have been the greatest genius of repetition in the history of music. For example, the small cell ♩ ♫ ♩ ♩ was so amply used in the classical period that one would think a composer of originality would have looked for something different. But Beethoven constructed page after page using nothing but this rhythmic motif. For example, in the *Allegretto* of the Seventh Symphony, he begins with twenty-four repetitions of this cell (Example 1(a), below) before giving any real change. Again, the same cell (in halved note-values, i.e. ♫ ♫ ♫ ♫) comprises almost the entire development section of the first movement of the 'Pastoral' Symphony, being repeated seventy-two times at one point, with hardly a break (Example 1(b), below).

Example 1a: Beethoven: Seventh Symphony, 2nd movt.

Example 1b: Beethoven: 'Pastoral' Symphony, 1st movt.

Of course, there is a secret to the success of such a seemingly mechanical process. Beethoven introduced change, not to such an extent that it would break the mood, but just enough to keep our interest alive. In the *Allegretto* the music begins in the sombre low register and gradually rises through the octaves. In addition, a prominent counter-melody is introduced (itself largely made up of the small cell of our example). There is nothing dramatic — it is all simple, yet effective. The example from the 'Pastoral' Symphony has even simpler means of change. The repetitions cover two areas, each of thirty-six bars. Each time the key changes (first up a third, then down a third) and there is a gradual *crescendo* and *diminuendo*. Very slender ideas with which to cover such large areas, very slender indeed, but nobody has ever complained of monotony; rather we are filled with wonder by an experience so moving and poetic. To sum up: don't be afraid of repetition, but do use a degree of change, enough to suit the mood and effect you wish to create.

This brings us to an allied formal factor — the rise and fall of emotion through a musical section. If the emotive flow is too even, interest will lapse; if changes of emotion are too abrupt, the unity will be destroyed. The ebb and flow of emotion should therefore be carefully controlled. (Of course this factor varies according to the character of the musical material: placid material calls for much less change than material which has a strong emotional urge.) One form in which we have not only change but contrast is variation form. While it is important for each variation to be constant in mood, it is of course necessary to have contrast between variations. We must plan the degree of contrast and the specific mood of each variation so that the overall contours of change in the piece as a whole follow a convincing emotive path. Obviously, the last part must have a sense of finality, but the emotion of each part of the work must have its proper place and be allied to what has gone before and what follows. Changes should not be too rapid or abrupt, for the effect can be incoherent and disorientating. (The last movement of Webern's Symphony Op. 21 comes to mind — a theme and variations. The theme and each variation are extremely brief, only eleven bars, and each finishes so quickly and changes mood so rapidly that at a first hearing one cannot possibly grasp the course of events. Indeed, after lecturing on this work for twenty-five years, and though I could write out most of it from visual memory, it still sounds elusive.)

This elusive quality is common to much modern music based on non-repetition — the complete avoidance of restatement of any specific feature. This does not mean that all formal principles have been abandoned — the form may be based on very logical mathematical principles, or on structures which are retrogrades or inversions of what has gone before (which makes the musical ideas themselves somewhat elusive) — but if there is no repetition of well-sculptured subject matter, the music is almost certain to escape the memory, even after several hearings. We are left only with the memory of fleeting colours, perhaps a small note-group which appears to be half-familiar (like something we have heard before), or some spectacular moment like the boom of a gong. But the memories are insubstantial and rapidly fade.

Is there any alternative? Probably not, if one insists absolutely on the principle of non-repetition. My own solution is a compromise: avoid precise repetition, but use enough repetitions with elements of change to keep the listener formally orientated and continuously interested.

We have already said that today's performers may be expected to improvise. Is it possible to observe formal principles with a mind preoccupied with spontaneous composition? It is certainly difficult to improvise well and keep to precise forms, because this means being able to remember and replay what we have played before. Nevertheless, it is important to achieve a semblance of coherent form. There are a few solutions, such as improvisation on a ground bass, on a theme, or using a skeleton harmonic framework as in jazz. Certainly many good jazz improvisers have a personal vocabulary of musical 'gestures' which they use every day. To make up an improvisation using this material is part of their trade, and their habit of working at a certain familiar phrase and making it develop and grow produces music which we can all grasp and remember, especially if we know the performer's style well. But though it may sound free and uninhibited, the skeleton framework of harmony or a theme, which can remain almost completely hidden, supports the whole and gives it its coherence.

Those who play aleatory music (where the composer may use only graphic signs, or may suggest certain note-groups, to be played in a certain way, or even perhaps as the player wishes) may also have a stock-in-trade of musical gestures which will help them produce a convincing result in any situation.

Sometimes organists or other solo instrumentalists have to make up their own music at a moment's notice. It is a necessary way of life for many of us. How is it best done? It is all too easy to fall into the trap of wandering on, following the whim of the moment, chopping and changing from sombre meditations to joyous paeans. To the listener, such music is incoherent and formless. One way to avoid this is to think for a moment before beginning, searching for some idea, however brief, on which our imagination can work. If we use the art of repetition and change, this small idea can then grow and help make all the music, or at least enough of it to generate a formal logic, a compelling emotional experience for those who listen. With the experience of almost fifty years, I find improvisation easier than reading music. But how many dull moments may I have given my listeners? It is important in composition to be intensely self-critical, but to be self-critical while improvising is a difficult task indeed.

A word about musical form and numbers. Though it is too early for beginners to concern themselves with the relationship between musical forms and mathematics, the often surprising exactness in the relative proportions of musical sections, and even between movements, may be mentioned here. Sometimes the relationship is obvious, as in Alban Berg's Lyric Suite, where the number of beats and bars, even metronome indications, are largely based on the number 23 and its multiples. Berg worked out his proportions deliberately, by design, in the same way as other composers have done in some periods since the Middle Ages. But it is surprising how many works by composers such as Schubert and Beethoven, who probably never dreamed of creating mathematical proportions, have a degree of exactness in the relative length of sections of movements. It must be that good musical form depends for its success not only on the principle of statement and change, but also on the proportions of one musical period in relation to another, and also to the whole of a movement, perhaps even to the whole of a multi-movement piece. But though this supposition may be fairly accurate, it can certainly be stated that a slavish adherence to principles of precise proportions cannot in itself be an absolute guarantee of good musical form, which, as we have stressed again and again, depends on the satisfaction of psychological and emotional needs. However, as I have said, this proportional factor is too abstruse for beginners to consider, even though for more mature composers it may well be an abiding concern.

4 Melody

For me, melody is the most important factor in music. Sometimes, of course, harmony, texture, colour, or percussive rhythm may be the main elements of a work, but in general melody is supreme, dominating all other factors. We may sometimes hear merely a fragment of a melody, yet we know immediately what it is, where it comes from. Can we do this with harmony, texture, etc.? I think not.

I believe therefore that our music is to be recognized by its melodies, and that it is highly important that they be distinctive, with clear-cut, decisive shapes. For a melody to be memorable it does not need to be complex or extremely 'different'. It may be very simple and use ideas which other composers have also used. Many composers have used melodic shapes based on virtually the same scale and chord patterns, or on similar rhythms, yet produced themes unmistakably their own. Verdi is never mistaken for Wagner, nor Puccini for Tchaikovsky, because their melodies have personal distinguishing characteristics which make them instantly identifiable.

How can our melodies be made both memorable and distinctive? This is not easy to answer. Each of us speaks with his own voice, and though the tone may be rich or poor the voice is unique. Similarly, our melodies are our own, but they may be striking or mediocre according to some hidden talent or the lack of it.

There is no certain formula for making good, original melody, yet we can give some principles which will help towards this goal. Later we will discuss different technical constructions, but for the time being we will define precisely what makes melody, and what, probably, makes it distinctive.

Melody is a rise and fall of notes, related to each other in time. There are therefore two main melodic components:

(1) A pattern of notes, rising and falling.

(2) Rhythmic designs which relate the notes to one another in time.

In my opinion, distinctiveness and memorability owe more to rhythmic design than to pitch patterns. Example 2 gives two melodies, one based on chord patterns, the other on a descending scale with only one note omitted:

Example 2a: J. Strauss: *The Blue Danube*

Example 2b: Verdi: *La traviata*

The pitch material is almost trivial, yet in each case, after the first three or four notes, we can immediately recognize the melody. This is because the rhythmic designs, though not striking, give decisive shapes to the music. Without the rhythms, the melodies lose their identity.

On the other hand, we can take a well-known rhythm and change the notes, but the music will still be identifiable. Everyone will recognize Example 3 as the opening of Beethoven's Fifth Symphony, even with the altered notes.

Example 3

We may conclude that rhythmic shapes determine melodies more than do pitch patterns. This usually means that melody benefits if notes are of different durations. But how many student melodies are made up of even crotchets, with correspondingly dull results? Even the simple device of lengthening one note and shortening another can transform the music (as in Example 2(b), above).

Again, regarding memorability, it is important that note patterns and rhythms recur. The onward flow of music depends on the fulfilment of expectancy, on the recall of a note shape or rhythm which is already familiar. The moments of this recall are often quite predictable. For example, with music of the Mozart period we often know what is coming next, even on the first hearing of a work. Of course, this can lead to rather over-obvious themes, but this psychological necessity is a factor we cannot ignore. If we do the opposite, and write melodies which are always changing, we will find that by the end of the melody we will have forgotten the beginning. We will remember a general impression, but nothing definite. And yet many students fear that any form of repetition will be 'boring'.

It would be ideal if we could list the factors which make up a good melody. But as soon as we decide on a 'rule' there seems to be an outstanding exception to contradict it. However, an attempt must be made to make constructive suggestions, even if there are glaring contradictions.

Good melody is often the result of a mixture of various factors, which may be summarized as follows:

Distinctive rhythmic design. Regular movement tends towards monotony, giving the effect of a hymn-tune. If this even movement is only slightly broken, a well-sculptured melody can result:

Example 4: Musorgsky: *Pictures from an Exhibition*

If this melody were made up only of crotchets it would have no life; as it is, the occasional groups of two quavers give an impulse to the flow. Again, we can take a pattern of notes in chords which completely lack distinctive character:

Example 5

But with a decisive rhythm, the melody becomes vital:

Example 6: *La Marseillaise*

Note how irregularities of movement are frequent. Some music has a rich variety of movement, other music depends on very little change (as in the Musorgsky example shown above). Excessive variety of rhythm can produce lack of memorability (Example 7):

Example 7: Stravinsky: *Canticum sacrum*

Sur - ge a - qui - lo;   et   ve   -   ni, ve - ni, aus- ter;

per - fla,   per - fla hor - tum me - um,

Distinctive note patterns. These can be produced by a mixture of adjacent-note movement and leaps. Of course, much music has been composed using only scale and chord patterns, and if they have rhythmic distinction we may still find them useful. But if we wish to get away from such obvious, well-used material, we have to use the only alternative — a mixture of adjacent notes and wider intervals. This was of course Musorgsky's plan in Example 4. Avoid restricting the notes of a melody to a small area, as this can result in equally limited expression. Notice how the melody given in Example 8, after four bars of (almost) adjacent notes, suddenly expands into more intense emotion with the octave leap and the temporary abandonment of stepwise motion:

Example 8: Schumann: Piano Concerto Op. 54, 1st movt.

Allegro affettuoso

This shows leaps placed at the right psychological moment, when the intensity of a large leap is crucial to the emotional flow. Notice below (Example 9) how Ponchielli begins with small leaps and then, as the melody reaches its climax, expands to leaps of a fifth, a sixth, and a seventh before the theme sinks again to less emotional expression:

Example 9: Ponchielli: *Dance of the Hours (La Gioconda)*

High notes at climaxes. We have already shown above (Examples 8 and 9) how the highest note is reserved for the peak of emotion within a phrase. Similarly, in an extended theme, there will usually be one supreme climax, and once again the highest note is best reserved for that point. In Example 10 the high G is produced only in bar 29 (notice also the strongly emotive leaps around the climax point):

Example 10: Puccini: *La bohème*

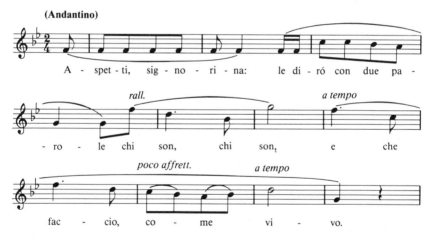

As a very general rule, one can observe that composers keep back climax points to the later part of melodic sentences and towards the end of complete themes. Good music resembles good speech: a sentence needs to work towards a main point and then decline before beginning again, while in a whole speech we have to prepare for and build towards the main point of the argument. Once this has been accomplished the speech may be rounded off fairly quickly, but not over-hastily. Music does just the same, though obviously points of high climax are by no means always needed. There are many pieces which avoid climaxes altogether, such as the Pastoral in Vivaldi's

'Spring' Concerto (*The Seasons*, Op. 8, No. 1). This master of tranquility uses only four adjacent notes in the first half of his melody.

Low notes. The lower notes of a melody are usually placed at points of emotive decline. However, some composers — Mozart is an example (cf. the Andante of his Piano Concerto K. 467 and that of his Clarinet Concerto) — may leap from a high register to a low one and back again, with great effect. This sudden use of low notes gives them prominence and unusual power. At the same time a change of register is always a relief, and a theme which is 'opened out' over a wide span has a greater emotional potential than one which stays in a small area.

Well-defined phrases. We never write words without using punctuation to form them into well-defined sentences. Without punctuation, reading becomes tiresome and the text incomprehensible. Music is the same. Each musical sentence should be well contained, with appropriately placed moments where the phrase rises, falls, or rests for a moment before moving on. The use of rests can be particularly telling, and a moment of silence can be even more poignant than sound, especially as a preparation for an effective utterance.

Without well-defined melodic periods phrases become inconclusive, merging into one another. The music wanders on, it is hard to tell the end of one phrase from the beginning of another, and the theme loses shape and becomes unmemorable.

The absence of rests can often give a dull, plodding effect, which even Bach could not avoid. In his Bourrée from the Lute Suite in E minor (Example 11, below) the music is made almost entirely of successions of two quavers and a crotchet without a single rest. This continuous movement was, of course, typical of bourrées and gavottes, and perhaps Bach was simply following a convention; none the less, the result it not very distinguished.

Harmonic suggestion. Some of the finest melodies give little hint of the harmonies that go with them. In writing tonal music there is therefore no need to be over-concerned with harmonic suggestion (introducing accidentals for modulations etc.). Accidentals are placed according to the emotional needs of the melody itself. When you come to harmonize these can then be treated either as chromatic appoggiaturas (or non-modulating substitution notes), or as modulating accidentals. However, as modulating notes (e.g. sharpened leading-notes) are particularly important at cadence points, it is well to provide for these in the melody.

In some music (e.g. the bourrée just mentioned) modulation is such a prominent feature — it relieves the monotony of excessive repetition — that inevitably the melody must be written with the underlying harmonies in mind. The same is true where harmonic colour is to be a prominent feature of the music. Harmony has a special fascination for many of us, but once again I would warn students against thinking of harmonies before they have conceived the melody. The theme must not lose its freedom of flight, or be allowed to decline into a secondary role, of inferior interest to the harmony.

In addition, students must be warned not to try to write complete harmony simultaneously with the melody. Many students tie themselves in knots in only four bars, and can then go no further because they have concentrated on complex harmonizations and ignored the thematic flow. The secret of continuity is in the melody, which they have barely considered.

Emotive contour. Every melody has its own emotive 'contour', and this should be roughly conceived from the start. Some melodies barely rise and fall in emotion, so their 'contour' would be almost level. These are usually in placid music such as the pastorales in Handel's *Messiah* and Corelli's 'Christmas' Concerto.

Very occasionally, music can move in successions of falling emotional curves, melodies beginning high up and gradually falling, as in Borodin's Polovtsian Dance in *Prince Igor*. More generally, music has emotive contours which rise and fall, often reaching the highest point towards the end of a melody. The degree of rise and fall depends on the relative intensity of emotive expression.

Normally, emotive intensity is achieved by:
Rapid movement
Increasing impetus
Strong rhythms
High notes
Increased volume

and emotive relaxation and decline by:

Less movement
Declining impetus
Weaker rhythms
Lower register
Decreased volume

Melodic construction

Many readers will be displeased to see 'construction' mentioned in connection with melody, regarding melody as something entirely inspired. Certainly some melodies are the result of pure inspiration, but more normally they are conceived in moments of clear vision, probably with only fragmentary suggestions. From such small beginnings the melody is completed through sheer hard work — helped (if we are lucky) by other occasional moments of intuition.

As one cannot induce inspiration (some have tried in vain, using drugs or alcohol), all we can do here is write about the 99% of work and skill which forms the other part of melody writing. Even the product of inspiration may need skilful pruning and reshaping. Beethoven's sketchbooks reveal how often his first visionary ideas were modified — chopping and changing until at last they fall into shapes of full significance.

Single-cell construction. We will begin by illustrating the simplest form of melodic construction, where the melody is formed entirely by repetitions of a small rhythmic cell ♫ ♩ (Example 11):

Example 11: Bach: Bourrée (Lute Suite in E Minor)

Example 11 is the first half of the melody, modulating from E minor to G. Notice how the melody, though apparently continuous, falls into four phrases, forming two main sentences. The rhythmic cell is departed from at only two points: the end, where longer notes give a moment of repose; and at mid-point (the end of the first sentence), where the two quavers of the motif are extended to six. This kind of multiplication of a brief cell is common to many melodies, for variety, added interest, or to give a moment of decline (as above). Notice too the melodic contour — two sections beginning high and falling to low points.

That this almost rudimentary form of melodic construction can give supremely expressive results is shown in the theme of Elgar's *Enigma Variations*, formed from the cell ♪ ♫ ♩ ♩ and its reversal ♪ ♩ ♩ ♫ (Example 12):

Example 12: Elgar: *Enigma Variations*

Notice the emotive contour: an expressive rise and fall, with the highest note and largest leaps at the most emotive point. The theme continues with four bars made entirely from the cell ♩ ♫ (part of the reversal of the original cell), concluding with an exact repetition of Example 12.

Notice also the poignant rests and clear sculpturing of each brief phrase. As the pitch patterns were presumably dictated by Elgar's 'secret' melody, we can safely assume that his invention, and indeed the beauty of his creation, lay almost entirely in his construction. Construction is therefore to be valued (rather than despised) for its fruitful possibilities. The works of Beethoven and Bach are full of similar constructions, and it is remarkable how certain basic rhythmic cells (such as ♩ ♫ ♩ ♩ or ♪ ♫ ♩ ♩) are used over and over again in their music.

Sometimes a cell will be used in augmented or diminished note-values, or an occasional note may be lengthened. In Example 13, from Schubert's Impromptu Op. 142 No. 3, one of the crotchets is lengthened in bar 2 (a common form of change), while in the last bar the rhythmic cell is diminished by halving the time-values. Such small changes are invaluable in giving themes renewed vitality, while at the same time preserving unity.

Example 13: Schubert: Impromptu Op. 142 No. 3

Multiple-cell structures. Composers often construct their basic phrases from several different cells, in order to have more variety of 'material' and produce music which is more subtly evolved and richly diversified. The use of several cells also gives greater possibilities of length, for there is less risk of repetitiousness. Alban Berg's Piano Sonata Op. 1 comprises a single long movement; it is almost continuously melodic, yet virtually the whole piece seems to be derived from rhythmic cells given out in the first phrase:

Example 14: Berg: Piano Sonata Op. 1

Notice how cells *a* and *c* are really the same, *c* being an augmentation of *a*. The five quavers of *b* are really an overlapping of two groups of three quavers: ♪♪♩ ♩ ♩. Three triplet quavers appear fairly early in the piece and then become a frequent feature, but of course these can be regarded as a diminution of cell *b* in its three-note form.

Berg makes frequent use of multiplying rhythms (♫₃ ♫₃ ♫₃ or ♫♩ · ♫♩ etc.) to form long, flowing phrases, but of course this proliferation of small cells is by no means new. It began long ago in the early Baroque era.

Melody through decoration. Themes with apparently quite varied and elaborate rhythmic outlines can be made by decorating a melody which in itself is quite simple, and which may conform to a well-known pattern. Bach's Sarabande from the E minor Lute Suite may at first seem to be a freely flowing melody; in reality, it is a skilful decoration of what was probably a simple basic conception:

Example 15: Bach: Sarabande (Lute Suite in E minor)

simplified design

The rhythm ♩ ♪ ♩ (bar 2) is really a diminution of ♩ ♩ ♩ (bar 4); the quavers in bar 1 are echoed in augmented values in bar 3; while the note succession in bar 1 is used again to form bars 3 and 4. This material forms the basis of the rest of the piece, with the addition of rapid scale passages based on diminutions of the quaver movement in bar 1. The decoration is therefore not quite as free as it looks, in reality forming part of an evolved construction.

Some of Bach's melodies, however, are so freely formed that it is impossible to decide whether, like the above Sarabande, they could have had a simple outline as their origin, or whether Bach followed a free vein of inspiration, ignoring a well-defined construction. A familiar example is the 'Air on the G String' (Air from the Third Orchestral Suite). This lovely melody follows first one pattern, then another, without establishing a precise thematic design. The result is a slightly elusive quality which is part of its singular attraction.

Melody by growth. In music of this century, composers have cultivated melodic 'growth' by choosing a specific group of notes, and then, by presenting them in different orders or different rhythmic shapes, created melody which proliferates from what may be only a very limited stock of initial material. In the following example from the organ pedal melody of the Entrée in Messiaen's *Messe de la Pentecôte*, only four pitches are used, yet the composer reshapes the rhythms and note-orders so skilfully that there is no feeling of repetitiousness or monotony:

Example 16: Messiaen: *Messe de la Pentecôte*

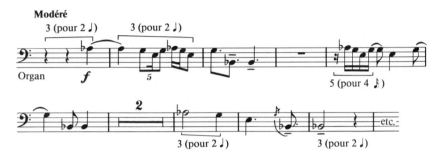

In Example 17, from the slow movement of Bartók's Fourth String Quartet, we have a wonderfully sweeping melody which seems to grow out of the first bar. At first there is only the hesitant semitone movement D♯ – D; then this expands to include tones and minor 3rds; then we have leaps over 5ths and 7ths. This growth in interval size is matched by growth in rhythmic propulsion, so that the whole eight-bar phrase seems a complete unity, growing from the small seed of the first two notes:

Example 17: Bartók: String Quartet, No. 4, 3rd movt.

Non-repetition. For the sake of completeness, we will give an example of melody in which there is neither repetition, of however small a component, nor evidence of any constructive factor. Everything is new, nothing is repeated or made to refer to what has gone before. Inevitably, nothing is memorable, or of great value. This is perhaps the result of a deliberately indifferent attitude by the composer, who says that the piece can be played by most instruments as a solo, or by groups of instruments as ensembles; that the general tempo can be between ♩=42 and 132, the duration between four and twelve minutes; and that the ordering of different melodic strands can be quite haphazard. In fact, as much is left to 'chance' as possible. Example 18 is one of the fifteen or so melodic fragments which make up the piece:

Example 18: Maderna: *Serenata per un Satellite*

Composing a complete melody

The first phrase. We have discussed different methods of melodic construction. Now we can begin on the first phrase — the most important of the whole theme, for the success of everything else depends upon it. The first phrase should have a distinctive and eminently memorable nature. The rhythmic design and pitch scheme are therefore extremely important.

The first phrase should be a complete musical thought which demands a response or 'reply' in the next phrase, to make up a complete 'sentence'. Usually it is a united group of notes, as in (a) below, but sometimes it can be broken up into two or more parts, as in (b):

Example 19a: Verdi: *I Lombardi*, Act IV

Example 19b: Tchaikovsky: Fifth Symphony, 3rd movt.

This first musical thought usually comprises an even number of bars, two, four, or even six, but there is nothing to prevent it being otherwise (note the eleven-beat phrase in the Musorgsky, Example 4, above). Today we tend towards irregularities, rejecting over-square rhythms and phrases. The important thing is that, regular or irregular, the first phrase should sound convincingly complete, yet must also demand another phrase in reply.

A word about the 'anacrusis'. The Verdi example above begins with an upbeat, or anacrusis. Many first phrases begin in this way, with a preparatory note or group of notes, and it is usual for each succeeding phrase to begin with a similar anacrusis. This is true only for music which moves in regular patterns, and we could well do otherwise if we wish.

Melodic continuity. Having discussed the construction of a melody's smallest essential part — the initial phrase — we can move on to the building of complete themes. Again, I would prefer to avoid laying down rules, which may prove inhibiting and a restriction on the imagination. This complete lack of rules will force us into a difficult situation, where the student will have to use his own intuition and aesthetic judgement. However, such a mental exercise may be found to be of more benefit to him than could any rules, and as such may not be such a bad thing.

Very often a student creates his first phrase and then finds himself at a loss. The trouble is that there are so many ways of continuing, so many alternatives and possibilities, that it would be wrong to advise him by saying that one procedure is better than another. On the other hand, it is our task here to make concrete suggestions as well as to stimulate ideas. Thus we may recognize a general classification of three kinds of melodic phrase:

(1) Phrases which demand continuity.

(2) Phrases which have a sense of temporary repose.

(3) Phrases which imply finality (in varying degrees).

Phrases of the first type correspond to a 'question' to which a phrase of the second type may provide an incomplete answer; a phrase of the third type gives a sense of completion. This is a rather naïve comparison with speech or writing, which do not necessarily move forward only by means of question and answer. However, the idea of one phrase 'replying' to another, or completing a 'sentence', is perfectly valid.

25

While we do not wish to get involved with harmonization at this point, it is important to point out that the above three kinds of phrases will probably have harmonic implications which contribute to their need for continuity, temporary repose, or complete finality. For instance, finality is felt in a return to the tonic, accompanied by tonic harmony, while temporary repose or the need for continuity is implied if the melody rests on another note with (inevitably) harmony which is not tonic harmony. Such factors, however, will be felt instinctively by any student with musicianship, and there is no need to quote such text-book rules as: 'Tunes will consist of two phrases. The first will end on any note except *doh*, the second must end on *doh*.'

To return to the problem of how to continue the theme after the first phrase is formed: the simplest solution is to repeat the first phrase exactly as it is. This kind of repetition has been a method of construction used by composers from Franck, through the French Impressionists, to such as Delius and Lennox Berkeley, and Ravel found it so fruitful that phrase repetition runs through entire movements of his music:

Example 20: Ravel: Sonatine for piano, 3rd movt.

In this example the melody does not change on repetition, and Ravel uses the technique to create a series of semi-static periods.

In Example 21, Franck gives an almost identical repeat of his first phrase (bars 1 and 2), with just enough change to satisfy a forward harmonic movement which is stronger than that in the Ravel. Notice how bars 5 and 6 are also identical:

Example 21: Franck: Sonata for Violin and Piano, 1st movt.

Another simple way to continue a theme is to use exactly the same phrase, but beginning on another note, usually higher. (Raising the pitch of a phrase creates heightened interest; lowering it generally causes a fall-off in intensity and a decline in interest.) In Example 22 Franck repeats his first sub-phrase (the first two bars) by raising its first note by a minor 3rd; he then repeats the process. This inevitably causes modulations, but the effect is to stretch out the sense of 'questioning' over the whole sentence, so that it is resolved only in bar 9.

Example 22: Franck: *idem*

A more frequent way of theme continuation is to repeat with some change — not the slight degree of change we have shown above, but the alteration of part of the theme to present even greater interest:

Example 23: Schubert: Entracte from *Rosamunde*

In this example, the second four bars have added interest as a result of various factors: larger leaps, higher notes, syncopation, modulation, increase in overall span, etc.

Here the element of change is contained within a repetition of the original phrase idea. In Example 24 change is presented in different degrees. In the Tchaikovsky, the second phrase is not unlike the first. It contains similar rhythmic elements, but they are used in different ways. The element of change is therefore small, and the sense of unity — through similarities — considerable. In the Weber, change is greater. The leaps of the first phrase, with their chordal implications; change into a falling scale pattern, while the impulsive, *staccato* dotted rhythm changes to a series of contrastingly smooth *legato* quaver runs, quite different in character:

Example 24a: Tchaikovsky: *Nutcracker Suite*, Danse de la Fée-Dragée

Example 24b: Weber: *Invitation to the Dance* Op. 65 for Pianoforte

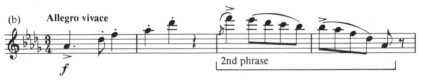

In the March from *Aida* (Example 25), after a rather long first phrase of three bars, there is a complete change to material which has never been used before. The element of change is considerable, but Verdi then makes use of segments of both phrases in close association for the rest of the theme.

To sum up this section, we can say that the first phrase of a theme may be followed by a second phrase to make a complete sentence, either through exact repetition, or by various degrees of change which can extend to the introduction of completely new material. No one procedure can be said to be absolutely right, and composers have used every compromise between these two extremes. All we can say is that each theme demands its own particular treatment, and that however much change is introduced there should be a convincing sense of unity. Change without unity would lead to disruption and chaos.

Example 25: Verdi: *Aida*, Act II

The second sentence. Having formed the first phrase and its complement as the first sentence of our theme, we must turn to the problem of what to do in the second sentence. First of all, how many bars have we written so far? Probably not many, perhaps no more than four. Surely this is too early to embark on new ideas — obscuring what we have so painstakingly created. In fact the listener is probably in just the right psychological state of expectation to hear again what he has just heard (or a slight variation of it). Yet it is precisely at this point that students — afraid of boring us with repetition — search for new material, abandoning their first ideas perhaps for the rest of the piece.

The second sentence will therefore in all probability use the material of the first. Often it will be completely identical, but in general it will tend to end with finality and with an added touch of interest (e.g. quicker movement, reaching a greater height, using larger leaps, etc.). Example 26 gives the first two sentences from the Andante of Mozart's *Eine Kleine Nachtmusik*:

Example 26: Mozart: *Eine Kleine Nachtmusik*, K. 525

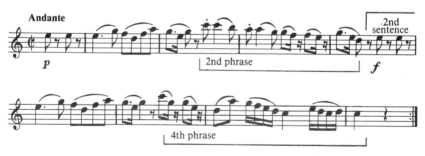

Notice how the second sentence uses material — semiquaver runs and larger leaps — not found in the first. We can see also how the first sentence has a second phrase using syncopation, which is a distinct change from the first phrase. Note too how the first sentence rests on D (part of the dominant chord), thus inviting continuation, while the second ends on C, confirming finality.

At this point, having reached the end of the 'second sentence', we can confirm that all the conventional classical music examined seems to be built in sentences, each of which comprises two phrases of the 'question and answer' type. There is always a first sentence in which the first phrase demands continuity, the second then providing repose. Further, in all the music examined, a second sentence, similarly made of two phrases, always comes to a point of temporary finality. (This double-sentence structure will be obvious from our analysis of thematic forms at the end of this chapter.)

We could therefore make a rule that 'melodies should begin with two sentences, each comprising two phrases etc.', but we must refrain from doing so. Many melodies of the last hundred years could not possibly be made to fit into such a restrictive rule − in fact many of us would avoid the feeling of regularity and 'squareness' that such a classical scheme produces. In the past, too, there were exceptions. For example, Vivaldi liked to use three-phrase sentences.

Contrast or repetition? Having reached the end of the second sentence, we have to decide whether to repeat what we have already written, or introduce something new as a contrast or relief. Classical composers at this point often took repetition so much for granted that they merely indicated an exact repetition with repeat marks (as in the Mozart above). We could do the same, but every piece of music must have its own shape, and many composers introduce new material at this point, even if only for a brief few bars.

The problem is this: should new material be similar to the old, or be in moderate contrast, or be extremely different? There is no simple answer. It must not be so different that unity is destroyed, or so similar that it gives no feeling of change. Some composers can introduce considerable contrast without destroying unity. In his famous 'Minuet in G' Beethoven introduces a third sentence (after repeating the first two) which seems to belong to a different world, yet is perfectly apt:

Example 27: Beethoven: *Minuet in G*

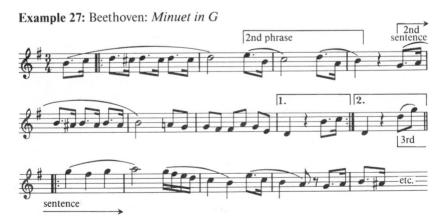

On the other hand, often a 'contrasting section' is made from existing material, creating a feeling of newness and freshness despite the apparent repetition. An example may be found in Mozart's third sentence from the Andante just quoted:

Example 28: Mozart: *Eine Kleine Nachtmusik*, K. 525

This looks quite different from the previous section (Example 26), yet it is really made up of semiquaver groups which end the second sentence, with the addition of the dotted rhythm which begins the second full bar of the music. It therefore contains nothing really new, but creates a pleasant feeling of freshness and change.

How long should the contrasting third sentence be? In order to provide an adequate period of relief it should be at least as long as the first sentence of the theme. We frequently find it comprises twice as much. But if it becomes too long there is a danger that the listener will forget the original theme, concentrating on the third sentence because it assumes too much importance. It should therefore remain within limited proportions.

Continuing the theme. After a contrasting period (the third, or the third and fourth sentences) it is most likely that we will return to the original theme. Any new thematic material at this point would lead to confusion. The unity of the theme is at stake, so that after a period of change it is inevitable that we return to our original discourse. This has been the method used by all the great melody-writers over several centuries. The length of the restatement of the first theme may be short or long, according to circumstances. For example, a short recall of the original theme (perhaps using only one sentence) would be sufficient if we wanted to continue the theme by introducing yet another period of change. But if we want to give a definite end to the melody we can bring in a more complete restatement of the original theme.

At this point we must therefore consider the shape of the entire thematic form, and illustrate various possibilities.

Complete melodic forms. Though we have so far considered writing a melody phrase by phrase and sentence by sentence (because it has been necessary to consider the small detail), a composer would be wise to avoid this step-by-step method. He would be working in the dark on two main issues: the total length of the complete theme, and the final form of his music. It is most necessary, before we begin, to have some idea of the skeleton framework which will shape the theme and create its total form. Length will depend on two factors, sentence length and the existence of periods of contrast. Short sentences can produce only short themes. Long sentences, which can stand plenty of repetition or extension, will make for long themes. A limited number of periods of contrast will make for brevity; adequate periods can lead to long themes.

We can best conclude our discussion of melodic construction by giving the skeleton form — sentence by sentence — of a number of melodies, showing how the principle of 'statement and change' (discussed in chapter 3) can be applied to theme building. The following symbols will be used:

A = first sentence, demanding continuation.
A^+ = as A but with change (added interest) or finality.
B = contrasting sentence, with or without finality.
C = sentence of further contrast to A, A^+, and B.

The number of bars in each sentence will be shown by numbers. (Some sentences overlap bars, beginning with an anacrusis which may occupy several beats, but with a correspondingly shorter last bar. These are rounded off to the nearest number of complete bars.)

The form of the melody of the Chopin Nocturne shown below is very common. Both the A^+ parts are highly decorated versions of A.

Chopin: Nocturne Op. 9 No. 2, for piano.

A A^+ B A^+
8 8 8 8 (32 bars)

Mozart: Andante from *Eine Kleine Nachtmusik*, K. 525 (see also Examples 26 and 28).

‖: A A^+ :‖ B A^+ :‖ A A^+
4 4   4 4   4 4 (40 bars)

The Mozart shown beneath the Chopin has the same form, using repetition and ending with a recall of the first section.

There follows a number of examples using forms which are slight extensions of those just discussed:

Beethoven: *Ode to Joy*, Ninth Symphony.

A A^+ B A^+ B A^+
4 4 4 4 4 4 (24 bars)

Tchaikovsky: Andante from the 'Pathetic' Symphony.

A A B A B A
2 2 2 2 2 2 (12 bars)

Schumann: *The Happy Shepherd.*

A A B A B A
4 4 2 4 2 4 (20 bars)

Chopin: Fantasia for piano.

A A⁺ B A⁺ B A⁺
8 8 4 8 4 9 (41 bars)

All these alternate change and restatement of the theme, once it is well established. Note that the first statement of the theme is always at least a third as long as the whole, while contrasting sentences are never very prolonged, and are sometimes quite brief.

The following is a more evolved extension of the above plan:

Brahms: Waltz Op. 39 No. 15.

A A⁺ ‖ B A A⁺ B A A⁺
4 4   6 4 4 6 4 4 (44 bars)

Finally, here are examples which use three different kinds of thematic material, all by Italians. Italians generally tend to be more liberal in their use of thematic material than other musicians. Each piece quoted here ends with new material, in each case giving added force and brilliance to the ending of operatic arias:

Verdi: 'La donna è mobile' from *Rigoletto.*

‖ A A B C ‖
   8 8 8 8   (68 bars)

Verdi: Brindisi from *La traviata.*

‖ A A⁺ B B A⁺ ‖ C
  10 10 8 8 10   14 (106 bars)

Bellini: 'Casta Diva' from *Norma.*

A A⁺ B C
4 4 4 4 (16 bars)

It must be stressed that these examples refer in some cases to complete pieces of music, in others to themes which form only part of a longer movement. However, the same principles apply in all cases, and as long as the music is primarily melodic, the various sections of large movements can be created with the melody-building methods we have described.

It will be noted that 20th-century music is hardly quoted. This is because the greatest melody-writers belong to past epochs and set an example which modern composers can hardly match. Also, even when modern composers do write melody, it is rarely presented in a straightforward way which can be regarded as a model. If a contemporary composer writes melody at all, it is usually complex, disturbed by interruptions, counterpoints, and 'effects', as if the composer prefers obscurity to simple clarity. Genius was once expressed through clarity and simplicity, and perhaps we are wrong to fear simplicity today.

Contemporary melody. The melody we have discussed in this chapter has been almost exclusively of a classical type. More modern usages will be summed up later in Chapter 12. At present the necessary technical background has yet to be investigated. However, a knowledge of classical melodic structures will still be useful, even if our purpose is to write music of a more up-to-date character.

Symphonic melody. In general, we have been writing about those melodies which are complete and have a well-defined entirety. However, it is important to observe that in many symphonies and in a good deal of chamber music a different situation prevails. Many movements (especially first movements) begin with very promising melodies (e.g. the 'Pastoral', the 'Eroica', etc.) which soon disappear like smoke in the wind, to be taken up again and worked over later on but which none the less fail to become complete. The reason is not easy to define, but it would seem that especially in first-movement, or 'sonata', forms composers have preferred to avoid extended melodies, resorting instead to short thematic ideas which are quickly displaced by other material. Sometimes this material may be a reworking of the original theme in a concentrated, active, and closely-knit symphonic texture. Just as often it may be new material altogether, in a bridge passage leading to new themes in the second subject group. Sometimes, as in Mozart, the bridge passage will occur very soon, and may be longer than the theme itself. In some cases, if there is no repeat of the exposition, the first theme may not be heard again until the recapitulation, by which time it may be almost forgotten. However, this is not a study of symphonic forms, and our sole purpose is to indicate the situation.

Other movements in symphonies and chamber music may have a much greater degree of completeness in their melodies, especially slow movements and dance pieces such as minuets and scherzos. It would seem that composers have preferred to be formally more complex in first movements. Part of the process has been to leave melodies incomplete, in an enigmatic and obscure fashion, sacrificing them to the technical prowess of symphonic 'textures' which perhaps have a greater degree of interest and a more intellectually appealing complexity.

5 Harmony and counterpoint

Harmony

A book on composition bases itself on the assumption that the reader is already familiar with conventional harmonic principles. However, it has been my experience that composition students do not sufficiently exploit their harmonic knowledge, often using only a limited vocabulary. Later, we will be looking at ways of expanding our vocabulary in adventurous ways, but for the moment I would like to make recommendations based on my observations over many years of student limitations, mainly in a diatonic field. We will be dealing with more chromatic harmony later on, in Chapter 10.

I believe harmonic poverty is often caused by a student's perfectly natural inability to think of more than one thing at a time. So I repeat: write a melody first, then harmonize it later. Many poor harmonizations are written because the student is trying to think of melody and harmony together, and inevitably both suffer in consequence. I have seen this kind of thing so often, and it will serve as an example to indicate at least five fundamental errors which are extremely common:

Example 29

The principal errors are:

(1) Each melody note is separately harmonized, and the result is a stodgy, unflowing harmonic and rhythmic movement.
(2) Only three chords are used: tonic, dominant, and subdominant.
(3) All chords are in root position. The rich effect of inversions has been ignored.

(4) There is no special interest in lower parts.

(5) Chords are bunched in the same area, instead of spreading and contracting purposefully. (The spread of notes is not too bad here. One often sees much worse bunching than this, where notes hardly have room to move.)

Example 30 reveals the fine harmonic quality of Grieg's original:

Example 30: Grieg: Sarabande *Holberg Suite*

(1) The movement of melody and harmony do not coincide (except towards the end). Their independence adds considerably to the interest.

(2) Different chords abound.

(3) Root positions of tonic, dominant, and subdominant are largely avoided. Instead, we have richly varied inversions of seventh, ninth, and added sixth chords, first inversion of the subdominant, etc. This gives an attractive and powerful harmonic effect. Especially fascinating is the almost secretive way the harmony changes in the first bar.

(4) The bass line has a purposeful direction, mostly in contrary motion to the melody, and includes an effective chromaticism (which is really outside the diatonic confines we are discussing). Such contrary motion almost always gives a good effect.

(5) The span of the parts spreads and contracts effectively. (Unfortunately, the inner parts, especially the tenor, are uninteresting.)

It is surprising how few students realize the full potential of simple diatonic harmony, even after they have studied it at school and university. To those who harmonize with the meagre resources of tonic, dominant, and subdominant in root positions only, I would recommend abstinence from the use of these chords for a while, and concentration on the other part of the vast diatonic field which is actually available.

What is really available? With diatonic triads, in root position and first and second inversions, we have a choice of twenty-one different chords (Example 31):

Example 31

If to these triads we add the possible inversions of added sixth and seventh chords, we have a choice of seventy different chords (not seventy-seven, as one would suppose, for some are duplicates):

Example 32

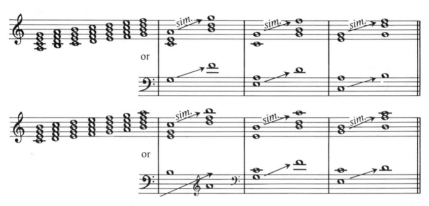

Add to this the fact that the notes in each chord can be varied in register (that chords can be 'close' or 'open'), and we have a very wide range of possibilities — and this with chords only in the key of C major. This chordal range is much wider than many students tend to use. If only they would avoid the root positions of the usual three chords, they would begin to discover what resources are available, especially if they realize that chords can often comprise four different notes (at least) instead of the usual three. Example 33 shows John Ireland's resources in using diatonic four-note chords when many triads have added notes of various kinds (6ths, 7ths, etc.):

Example 33: Ireland: *The Hills* for Choir

Ex. 33: (*cont.*)

green, How green and white and gold - en in the sum - mer light.

A word about dissonances. There are various ways of treating these, some conventional (and therefore perhaps a little banal), others more subtle, even engagingly surprising in their unexpectedness. There are four general ways of treating dissonances, which we will illustrate in the Karg-Elert Organ Interlude No. 11, quoted in Example 34:

Example 34: Karg-Elert: *Organ Interludes*

(1) Dissonant notes resolve conventionally by falling or rising to form part of a new chord — the expected resolution (e.g. dominant–tonic) — as at ① in Example 34, where the progression is D (first inversion) to G. The 7th (C) falls to the new 3rd; the 9th (E) to the new 5th.

(2) Dissonant notes resolve in a conventional way, only to become part of an unexpected chord as in ②. The 7th, D, falls to C as part of the chord of F instead of the expected A minor.

(3) Dissonant notes do not resolve, but leap away to a consonance in the same chord, as at ③.

(4) Dissonant notes do not resolve but move to another dissonance (in the same chord, or a different one). There is no example of this in the Karg-Elert example, but it will be dealt with more thoroughly later when we discuss the style of free diatonicism.

It is important to establish exactly what degree of dissonance we want in our music, and how frequently it should occur — in other words to ensure that the harmonic style and atmosphere are consistent. Otherwise there is a danger that dissonance may be out of place, or be excessive for the context, or may occur at unexpected moments in a different harmonic mood. Dissonance is most powerful in a generally consonant context — hence the need to be extremely cautious in its use. Note how, in the Karg-Elert example, dissonances are fairly evenly spread, allowing a specific harmonic style which is rich and smooth, without unwelcome or joltingly unexpected events.

When harmonizing a piece we must decide what kind of horizontal spread we would like in the harmonic atmosphere. Do we want to create a restless mood, or a calm, pacific one? In the Karg-Elert example there is a restless harmonic change on every beat until the final bars, which, needing a mood of repose, change chord only twice a bar. If we wished for a more restful effect we could use far less harmonic change, holding chords for several beats (Example 35):

Example 35

This shows how a broad area of melody can be accompanied by the same harmony. There is absolutely no need to change harmony each beat, or even frequently. The melody of the Adagio from Dvořák's 'New World' Symphony owes its air of peace largely to the static harmony, which begins to move beat by beat only when there is a climax. After the climax repose is again created by returning to very unfrequent harmonic change. On the other hand, if one wants a mood of restlessness or disquiet, frequent harmonic change (and dissonance) is exactly what is needed. However, in some situations the melody is so pacific and widely spread that harmonic change can be relatively frequent, embroidering but not changing excessively the atmosphere. In Example 36 movement is maintained not only rhythmically, but also by harmonic changes which justify the rhythmic designs; these would otherwise have a less constructive significance (see next page).

Modulations. It is important to establish the harmonic character of our music from the beginning. Is it mainly diatonic or chromatic? Will it modulate or not? If it is diatonic we may never need to modulate at all. It can also be highly chromatic without introducing any well-defined modulations which establish clear tonal areas.

Example 36: Bach: Chorale Prelude *Durch Adam's Fall* (Organ)

If we have decided on a moderate degree of modulation, it is well to know what is most effective and what subsequent progressions (to return to the tonic) are good. It is best to write what sounds smooth and natural, so we should forget about modulations to far-distant keys (e.g. C to F♯). To get there would be a rough passage, and the return tortuous. In some music this strained atmosphere may be just what we want, but for the moment our objective is rather to achieve a smooth, natural-sounding discourse.

Modulations towards keys on the sharp side of the 'circle of fifths' are good, providing they do not go too far. Supposing we are in C major we can modulate (taking in turn relative degrees of sharpness) to G, D (or D minor), A (or A minor), and E (or E minor), still with the prospect of an easy return to C; B would be too far. In fact we can go from C to any of the above keys without even modulating first, as long as the return is well made. For instance, the following chord progression is fluent, and often used:

C – E – A minor – D minor – G (7) – C

After the sudden jump to E, the remaining chords (including their versions with the 7th) all form part of the tonality of C, so that the harmonic journey is very smooth and has an air of inevitability. Similarly, all the following modulations are easy and effective:

C – D – G (7) – C
C – D minor – G (7) – C
C – A – D (minor) – G (7) – C
C – A minor – D minor – G (7) – C
C – E minor – A minor – D minor – G (7) – C

Modulation to the relative minor (included above) is common enough, and indeed an entire passage in the relative minor may be complete in itself (as a separate section of a movement), and need not be preceded or concluded with a modulation.

Modulation to keys on the flat side is usually limited only to the subdominant,[1] so that a chord progression something like the following is used:

C – C7 – F – D minor – G (7) – C

Many pieces of music employ in turn each of these three 'directions' of modulations: (1) towards sharp keys; (2) to the relative minor; and (3) towards the subdominant. Others omit the relative minor zone, moving first towards sharper keys, then towards the subdominant. Yet others have only an interlude in the relative minor between two sections in the tonic.

Modulations can therefore follow various routes, and it would be folly to recommend any particular pattern. It has been our purpose here to indicate what has been successful in the past, and the strong technical basis which underpins success. Even if we decide to do very differently, a knowledge of what has been strong and efficient elsewhere can guide us towards good results.

We have mentioned very little about harmonic paths in minor keys, but those with a sound harmonic upbringing will find it somewhat repetitive and superfluous to go over the whole ground again. What we have said about modulations in major keys can easily be applied to minor keys, with a little common sense.

Harmonic schemes on a larger scale, spanning large movements or in successions of movements, also require planning, for some change of key over a large area is needed to create contrast and relief. Within a large movement it is usual to establish one main key for the whole piece, but to have one or more separate sections in harmonic contrast. Each section would have its own tonality, usually related to the original key but sufficiently different to be noticeable. Suitable keys could be the relative minor (or major), the subdominant, or a key at a distance of a major or minor third above or below the original key (if a very notable contrast is needed). In the case of a number of movements it is usual, after a movement in a contrasting key, to return to one in the tonic. But this seems to be bowing to convention. Some composers have

---

[1] Modulations to still flatter keys are certainly possible, and can be very effective. For instance, the progression C – E♭ – A♭ – G – C sounds very well indeed, but its use is rare compared with the normal modulations discussed here.

instead made adventurous excursions, ending up quite successfully in a key other than the original tonic. There seems no reason why this cannot be done, as long as the key relationship between movements is good and logical. Much depends on the kind of harmony used. If it is very diatonic, our memory of the tonic key is not disrupted, and so it is important to preserve correct key relationships. If, however, the music is highly chromatic, our memory of the original key is quickly obscured, so that we accept the establishment of new keys readily and are not disturbed if the music ends in a tonality which has nothing to do with the original key.

Above all, good harmony should have an air of inevitability. It should appear so perfect that it could not be otherwise, that any change would be unthinkable.

Counterpoint

Contrapuntal, or 'polyphonic' textures have the special objective of creating additional beauty in music through the movement of parts. However, we must beware of the illusion that counterpoint always enhances the beauty of music, or that it has an inherent aesthetic value of its own. This may not always be so — indeed, the exact opposite may be the case. For example, some of our greatest melodies are given settings of the greatest simplicity, and to add 'counterpoints' would rob the music of some of its beauty.

Melody and harmony alone can make complete beauty, but some composers such as Bach created their harmonic textures through counterpoints in such a way that the melodic and harmonic qualities were not reduced but enhanced. Not all of us have such skill.

These warnings against an excess of counterpoint are really concerned with emotive beauty in music. Counterpoint can have its own intellectual appeal — something quite different. However, we must again take care, for though we find pleasure in following intricate counterpoints, imitations, inversions, double canons, and fugues, it is fairly certain that to the ordinary listener such music is an enigmatic confusion. Counterpoints may therefore be counterproductive, especially if they are obscure. We should err on the side of restraint, rather than of excess.

Strictly speaking, counterpoint or polyphony means music in a number of parts, where the voices are independent but combine to form a coherent whole. Normally there is some relationship between the parts, for if they are all different the result is incoherent (though a melody may have a countermelody with different characteristics). Contrapuntal music is usually therefore based on:

(1) Various voices, each using the same melodic outline.

(2) A principal melody, supported by contrapuntal voices which share other thematic material.

Sometimes the polyphony is treated in a free manner, voices imitating each other loosely for a time and then taking a free course until imitations begin again. In *fugato*, for example, parts imitate each other only at certain strategic points. In Renaissance polyphony voices were not always closely related, and thematic material could give way to other motifs as the work progressed. On the other hand, in canon and fugue imitations may be very precise and, especially with canons, continue strictly throughout the composition.

It is important to recognize that imitations may be 'true' as to intervals, or 'false'. In the canon at the 7th given in Example 37 Bach had to change the intervals of the following, or 'consequent', voice. Tones may become semitones, or vice versa, and 3rds be major or minor, according to the needs of tonality. If the upper part had been true as to intervals it would have been in B major, and of course the tonal results would have been chaotic:

Example 37: Bach: *Von Himmel hoch*

Var. III (free upper part omitted)

Organ

Whether intervals are true or false does not matter to listeners, who cannot easily distinguish the difference. However, composers often go to great pains to keep to true intervals. For example, in Variation 5 of the above-quoted work, Bach kept all intervals true in the successive canons by inversion at the 6th, 3rd, 2nd, and 9th — a Herculean task, and surely one which gave him some satisfaction.

Though a study of fugue is beyond the scope of this book, a brief illustration of various forms of canon will be useful, as this is the form of counterpoint most used, apart from free polyphony based on a lesser degree of imitation.

The most usual form is **canon at the unison,** or octave. This is also the easiest form to recognize. Example 38 shows a unison canon for two violins. The main theme is, however, in the bass — the so-called 'royal theme', said to have been invented by Frederick the Great of Prussia. This theme is used contrapuntally in other parts of the *Musical Offering*, but here it is the supporting voices which create polyphony. Example 38 is a 'perpetual canon' — in other words, the instruments can return again and again to the beginning, as in a round:

Example 38: Bach: *Musical Offering*

(Royal theme)

Canon at the octave or double octave is very similar to the above, but of course it is necessary to avoid crossing one voice below the bass. (This would happen if violin 2 in Example 38 were transposed an octave lower.) In the *Musical Offering* Bach writes a similar perpetual canon, with the 'royal theme' in the middle and two other voices, above and below, two octaves apart. In 'invertible counterpoint' the upper and lower voices can be reversed without loss of musical sense.

Canon can also be at other intervals, as mentioned in Variation 5 of *'Von Himmel hoch'*, above, but in tonal music the most usual interval, apart from the unison and octave, is canon at the 5th above or the 4th below. Thus canons often have tonic and dominant relationships, and in order to preserve a single tonality the 4th leap downwards from tonic to dominant often has to be followed by a leap of a 5th (dominant down to tonic). This kind of interval adjustment will be seen in Example 42, below.

Canon by inversion is not as easy to follow as normal imitation, and perhaps by reason of this obscurity it has been favoured by composers in this century — or at least by those who prefer obscurity to clarity. Example 39 is a canon by inversion at the 7th from Bach's *Musical Offering* in which the 'royal theme' is filled out with additional notes of a chromatic nature:

Example 39: Bach: *Musical Offering*

Royal theme

In the *Musical Offering* the degree of chromaticism is notable, and yet it is obvious that Bach's ideal was to use true intervals consistently, introducing a wide variety of modulation. It is possible that chromaticism favours the use of true intervals; certainly the high degree of chromaticism in serialism goes well with canonic usages.

Augmentation or **diminution** is used when one canonic voice moves slower or faster, respectively, than the other part or parts (which progress at the 'normal' speed):

Example 40: Bach: *Von Himmel hoch*

Var. IV

Organ

(free middle part omitted)

(In Example 40 a third free inner part is omitted for the sake of clarity. Eventually the music becomes four-part, when the pedal adds the chorale melody.) With augmentation it is obvious that the quicker-moving parts will end before the augmentation. In the above example the upper part ends the canon when the lower one is only at its mid-point, and then follows a free path. In other augmented canons it is common to repeat faster parts, so that all voices end together with the augmentation. The procedure with diminution is similar.

Crab canon, or **canon cancrizans,** is designed so that while the main voice moves forward the same part is played backwards. The mid-point is the most difficult to compose as the part writing, through using identical material, may be spoiled by stagnation. Example 41 gives the central four bars of the *canon cancrizans* in the *Musical Offering*:

Example 41: Bach: *Musical Offering*

The next example shows **double canon by inversion** from the Trio of the Minuet of Mozart's Serenade No. 12 (the entire piece is canonic). Here, two different canons sound simultaneously, and each is inverted:

Example 42: Mozart: Serenade No. 12

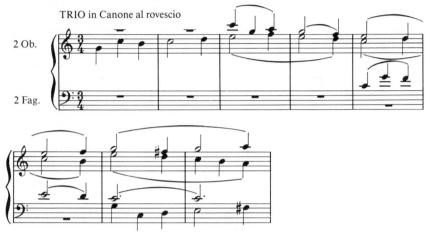

Notice how the intervals are not true, semitones often being imitated by tones and vice versa. The movement falls into two repeated halves, the second having more chromatic lower parts. So as to end each half-movement in four parts, the canons are not completed, the end of each section being free.

This free writing towards the end of movements or sections is common practice. If voices were to end at the same time as their canonic function ended they would fall out one by one, as in a round. Composers usually avoid this, writing free endings which are musically more satisfying.

The form of canons is important, especially if we want to avoid brevity. Length can be obtained by simple means: as one canon ends it can continue by voices changing roles — the following voice becoming the leading one — and perhaps register; the polyphony can be altered to canon by inversion, or the parts move backwards in retrograde or as a crab canon; we can have episodes where augmentation lengthens note-values or diminution shortens them, and towards the end a 'stretto' can bring imitations at closer intervals, giving a sense of culmination. Also, there is no reason why canonic sections cannot be separated by suitable interludes, possibly using homophony as a relief to polyphony, while the ending could be a non-canonic coda.

Writing canonic music is easier if we follow a golden rule: never go far with a leading voice without adding the consequent. For as soon as the consequent begins, it governs all that the leading voice can do. It is best to write no more than a bar of the leading voice before adding the consequent and assessing the result. If we follow this rule, most problems disappear.

We will be discussing contrapuntal writing again in Chapter 12. For the time being, I would like to repeat my warning against an excess of counterpoint. Inevitably, writing counterpoint has great intellectual appeal. It can be fascinating, but the allure of intellectualism can carry us away to the point of deliberately courting obscurity. I was once deceived as to the value of counterpoint. The first book I ever studied was Prout's *Strict Counterpoint*, which bestows on polyphony an aura of mysterious excellence. Then I saw that a D. Mus. degree required the composition of a fugue in eight parts, and when I wrote a Concerto for string orchestra I felt compelled to better this with a ten-part contrapuntal episode. This proved to be the worst part of the piece — dense, incomprehensible, and of no value. My ideas were readjusted as a result.

Above all, we must remember that music inclines more to emotion than to cerebralism. If we do write counterpoint, let it be lucid and expressive, like the lovely canon near the end of the Notturno of Borodin's String Quartet No. 2:

Example 43: Borodin: String Quartet No. 2

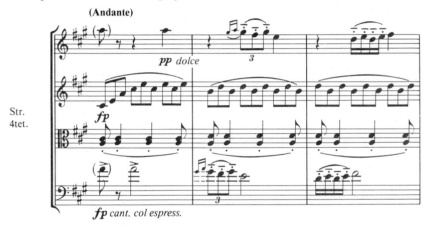

Here, the violin follows the cello like a mysterious echo, while the inner parts fill in the harmony very simply. It seems almost ingenuous, and there is no hint of intellectualism. Yet if we reflect a moment, we may realize that it is not so ingenuous after all. This canon did not appear by chance; it must already have been worked out when Borodin began the movement 110 bars previously. This is skill and forethought of a high order.

6 Vocal writing

'Song writers are born, not made.' While admitting the enormous truth of this statement, one could at the same time say that the number of song writers who never discover themselves is also enormous. Writing for the solo voice is such a daunting prospect that many composers never try it, and thus never discover their real potentialities.

Some composers — Beethoven was one of them — had little gift for vocal writing. Others excelled at it, and were indifferent with instruments. Certainly one must have a 'vocal' instinct, and to cultivate it, one must make an effort. Yet, if it is difficult to be a vocal composer, it is even more difficult to say what should be done. I am conscious that the most important thing is to be encouraging, to stimulate rather than to regulate. My comments are therefore not aimed at creating fixed rules, but at offering ideas.

The nature of words

Some words are already almost music:

'If music be the food of love — play on'

Shakespeare's words are already so musical that they can hardly be set to music. This is why musical settings of his Sonnets are amazingly few.

Other words have a completely different cast. They are narrative, and tell us of a situation, or prepare us for some significant message:

There were shepherds abiding in the fields,
keeping watch over their flocks by night.
And lo! the angel of the Lord came upon them,
and the glory of the Lord shone round about them,
and they were sore afraid.
And the angel said unto them,
Fear not; for behold! I bring you good tidings of great joy,
which shall be to all people;
For unto you is born this day, in the city of David,
a Saviour, which is Christ the Lord.
And suddenly there was with the angel a multitude of the heav'nly host, praising
God, and saying:

Once having told us the story, set the mood, and prepared us for the shout of a choir of angels, Handel could paint a triumphant musical fresco with just a few poetic words:

Glory to God in the highest,
and peace on earth.
Goodwill towards men.

Some words which narrate a story or describe a situation can be set in the form of musical prose and passed over fairly quickly, like the old recitative quoted above. Others have a higher poetry which expands the emotional feeling. These can be treated lyrically and, as in the old 'arias', dwelt on at length, even repeated to create bigger musical canvases. After all, Handel painted a great picture with only one word — 'Amen'.

This plan of alternating narrative and poetic lyricism was, of course, the outline scheme for many of the older operas, using recitative for the narration and arias or choruses to expand on the emotional and poetic episodes. More recent composers, such as Verdi and Puccini, have used the same scheme but with an 'arioso' narration more melodically defined and extended than was the old recitative. Other composers, such as Debussy and Janáĉek, so as to heighten the drama, have virtually abandoned aria and written continuous dramatic *arioso*, which hovers between narration and lyrical expansion as the situation demands. With less gifted composers this can result in opera which never becomes worth listening to, because the music never reaches and holds lyrical peaks. However, we are not concerned with opera here, but with words. I wish to make the student look again at the words he wishes to set. Are they narrative, or lyrical? If they are exclusively narrative they are useless for song writing. If they have adequately emotional words they can be used. But even with poems we have to be careful. Not all poems are sufficiently lyrical, and they may be overburdened with wordy information:

What faire pompe have I spide of glittering Ladies:
With locks sparkled abroad, and rosie Coronet
On their yvorie browes, trackt to the daintie thies
With roabs like *Amazons*, blew as Violet,
With gold Aiglets adornd, some in a changeable
Pale; with spangs wavering taught to be moveable.   (Chapman)

This kind poetry is far too prolix to be successfully set to music. It would be far preferable to use only a few words — a brief poem where every word is potent:

My love is like the grasses
    hidden in the deep mountain:
Tho' its abundance increases,
    there is none that knows.   (Ono No Yoshiki. 10th century)

50

Music has a time-span which is very different from that of speech — it spreads words into another time dimension, so that whereas a writer has to 'pad out' his thoughts to give his words extra body, such padding becomes burdensome in music — unwanted material we could well do without. So we should not hesitate to edit a text, cutting out what is superfluous, avoiding the padding, and retaining only the poetic essentials.

For instance, we may be setting Dryden's *Song for Saint Cecilia's Day* and wish to abbreviate the following verse by cutting out less important material:

What passion cannot Music raise and quell?
　When Jubal struck the chorded shell
　His listening brethren stood around,
　　And, wondering, on their faces fell
　To worship that celestial sound:
Less than a God they thought could not dwell
　　Within the hollow of that shell,
　　That spoke so sweetly, and so well,
What passion cannot Music raise and quell?

We could reduce this to the following, which retains the important parts of the above, keeps the message exactly the same, but brings it down to more manageable proportions from a musical standpoint:

What passion cannot Music raise and quell?
　When Jubal struck the shell
　His brethren on their faces fell
　　To worship that celestial sound.
Only a God could dwell
　　Within that sweet shell.

Form in vocal writing

Our first decision should be whether we want to write a traditional strophic song (each verse identical in length and metre), or music which is not chained to such a rigid form. With strophic song the musical form is very much governed by the poetic form. If we wish, we can establish one melody for the first verse and merely repeat it in the others, possibly varying some factor such as accompaniment, volume, colour, etc. Alternatively, we could make a more subtle form by using different music in one or two of the verses, alternating the musical setting to give a form such as ABABA or ABACA (supposing there are five verses).

In this traditional kind of song there is usually a well-defined tonal scheme, melodic phrases are symmetrical with repetitions of rhythmic outlines, and it is the melody which is all-important. As the same melody is used more than once for different words, no kind of 'word painting' can take place, for the notes which may be used for joy in one verse may be needed for melancholy in another. The melody and accompaniment can express the general atmosphere of the poem, but cannot underline the significance of individual words.

If we decide that this traditional strophic form does not suit our needs, we have the more difficult alternative of a looser form, in which the words are given more importance, while the music, intensifying their meaning and emotion, may fall into a supporting role. True, the music can rise to great lyric moments, but it should be through the words and not in spite of them.

This is where the difference between narrative and lyrical words comes out. The form of the music will be determined by the emotive peaks of poetic words and the valleys of narration. Formally, this could mean that there is continuous change, the music varying just as the words do. The results may be mediocre, because continuous change results in lack of memorability. We should seek to retain some definition in form by re-using certain melodic shapes, repeating certain note-successions or rhythms, perhaps even re-quoting an entire section which gives the main message of the work.

Many modern composers have avoided repetition, allowing the words to take the whole burden of form, carrying the music forward in an interminable wandering from one emotive crisis to another. At each moment the effect may be intensely impressive, but if we cannot remember anything with precision afterwards, the music is lost again forever, and its value is therefore diminished. It is surely preferable to retain some defined elements of musical form, so that the music can be retained in the memory.

Vocal music poses difficult problems in this factor of form. One can by no means lay down rules, and every composer must find his own solution. Perhaps Puccini discovered part of the secret of including a degree of narration within a melodic framework which could be called an 'aria' without upsetting the melodic and formal definition of the music. He had a great genius, first of all, for making a kind of recitative fit into the characteristics of his aria style. One of his best known, most poetic pieces — 'Che gelida manina!' from *La bohème* — begins with a kind of recitation of nine syllables on the same note, before the melody gets into flight. But more striking still is his ability to make the voice switch from aria to narration, at almost any moment, in such a way that we hardly notice it, because the orchestra takes over the melody from the singer. Example 44 is from 'Vissi d'arte' in *Tosca* at a point where the orchestra plays the melody (small notes) while the singer weaves a web of narration in different ways — reciting, joining the orchestral melody, forming a decorative counter-melody, etc. — all within the space of a few bars:

Example 44: Puccini: *Tosca*

(Lento) Die - di gio - iel - li del-la Ma-don - na al man - to, e die - di il

Voice and
orchertra

(Orch.)

can - to agli astri, al ciel, che ne ridean più bel - li. Nel - l'o - ra del do - lor per -

chè, per - chè, Sig - nor   ah,

etc.

There is great skill here, yet nobody seems to have recognized it for what it really is — the solution for preserving melodic and formal unity while at the same time using words with freedom and flexibility. Finally, we would stress that it is the musical values of vocal music which in the end have dominating importance, and therefore the musical form cannot be allowed to weaken in favour of literary factors.

Verse metre and musical metre

If we were setting a nursery rhyme to music, it would be quite appropriate to use the verse metre and rhythms also in the music; the result would be simple and naïve. 'Humpty dumpty' has a 6/8 metre in both the words and the music, and the match is perfect. But in music and poetry which aims at a higher aesthetic we have to avoid the trite effect which can result when words and music are in the same metre and move in identical rhythms. For instance, Wordsworth's famous poem 'My heart leaps up' is in 6/8 metre, and one could quite easily fit it to the 6/8 tune of 'Jack and Jill':

Example 45

My heart leaps up when I   be - hold a   rain - bow in   the   sky:

Of course, the result is horrific. To prevent this kind of puerile triteness, it is best to use musical metres which break across the verse metre, and in Example 46 a much more subtle effect is obtained:

Example 46a

Example 46b

The first version, (a) is more 'square' in rhythm than is (b), and therefore has less poetic potential. Note that as 'rainbow' is regarded as being the most important word it has the highest pitch. In (b) other important words such as 'I' and 'sky' are also given prominent places. The leap 'up' is given its musical place in both versions. (We will discuss this factor of word stress later.)

Before leaving this section on metre, it must be pointed out that a musical setting could be written which deliberately avoided any metrical pulse at all. Some composers feel that the use of obvious metres does not suit their own aesthetic, that metre is an impediment they can well do without. Wordsworth's poem could well be set as in Example 47:

Example 47

Of course, this kind of writing can be highly poetic, but there is also a danger of falling into aimless meandering, or of not being memorable precisely because it has no metrical background. Perhaps metre is one of the factors which help the mind retain sound patterns, and therefore aids the memory.

Word accentuation

In any poem or text, certain words have cardinal importance, some moderate importance, and others act merely as 'infilling' to complete the sense. If all words were set as if they were equally important, the main sense of the text would not be made sufficiently evident, and probably the music would lack decisive contours. In the Wordsworth poem mentioned in the previous section, several words could be regarded as important: 'heart', 'I', 'rainbow', and 'sky'. We have to make a choice. The melodic contour would suffer if we made them all equally prominent, so we have to decide on their relative importance and stress them accordingly.

A word can be made prominent by (1) giving it height and length; (2) being louder than words in the same phrase; or (3) being stressed by its position in the rhythmic design.

Conversely, less important words should be lower in pitch, relatively short in duration, given weaker dynamic values and placed in subordinate positions in a rhythmic design.

Melisma

The most poetic words in a text can be given more emotive power by using melisma. The most important vowel is set to two or more tied notes in a phrase designed to increase the lyrical expression (see Example 47, above). Alternatively, melisma may also be used for word painting. In Handel's 'Every valley' (*Messiah*) the 'crooked' path is illustrated by undulating melisma, and the rough places 'plain' by repetition of one level note.

Declamation

Narrative words can be passed over fairly quickly by declamation, which can vary between two extremes. The words may be recited in more or less regular durational values on one note, or the notes may change now and again. The result is mediocre and will probably sound somewhat churchified. Conversely, the note durations and rhythmic shapes can vary considerably, and if rising and falling note patterns are used a much more poetic and musical result is obtained, which can be close to *arioso*.

Climaxes

Every poem or text has its main point of climax, and probably several less important ones. In strophic songs, the climax points of the text may well not coincide with those of the music, especially if they are both conceived independently (which is usually the case). However, when music is written for a specific text, the maximum musical climax must be kept back for the decisive point in the words. Lesser peaks of musical interest will then coincide with textual climaxes of lower intensity. Naturally, the highest note is usually kept back for the greatest climax, together with maximum volume, note-length, accentuation, etc. It is rather important to prolong important climaxes, rather than let them slip away quickly, by holding them over an adequate period, through word repetition, musical extensions, etc. Of course, this kind of thing can become bombastic and rhetorical. Nevertheless, all struggles should have their recompense, and the effort laid out to achieve a satisfactory musical culmination would be in vain if the climax were to disappear before anyone really noticed it. The real point is that everything should be in proportion. If our style is reserved and peaceful, a gentle climax is enough, but if we are forceful and aggressive, it has to have much more duration, body, and weight.

Decorations

The voice is a flexible instrument, and in the past a singer was expected to decorate the music suitably and with taste, varying from the occasional grace-note or appoggiatura to effects of coloratura virtuosity. Nowadays such decorations are usually written out in the notation. Sometimes composers decorate their music to such a degree that it almost seems to be the main substance of the music. With composers such as Barraqué, Boulez, and Berio the singer has to display extreme virtuosity more or less continuously:

Example 48: Boulez: *Le Marteau sans Maître*

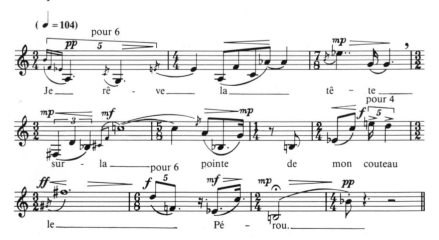

Sometimes decorations are most apt for painting the significance of special words which are central to the significance of the poem, or set its atmosphere. In Example 49, the melody not only illustrates the 'twining ropes of twisted vine', but also intensifies the poem's sense of uncanny desolation at nightfall:

Example 49: Smith Brindle: *Three Japanese Lyrics*

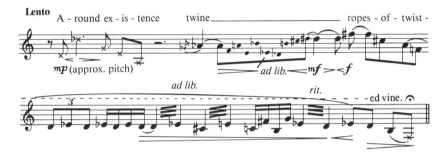

Vocal range

Many contemporary composers write for singers who have an exceptional range and absolute pitch. There has been a move towards a preference for flexible middle-range voices such as those mezzo-sopranos and baritones who can sing both quite high and quite low. But singers with this ability (and who also have absolute pitch) are not very common, and if we want to have our music sung by the majority of singers, it is best to write within the normal limits:

Example 50

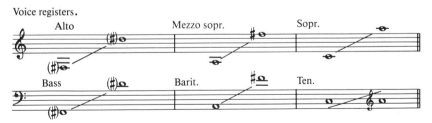

Many singers can exceed these limits, but we must remember that, apart from the fact that most people these days have middle-range voices, everyone has a limited zone in which the voice is at its best. This zone is usually in the upper-middle part of the voice, where the singer has power but does not tire so easily. Below this zone there is a fall-off in power and tone quality (especially with sopranos and tenors). Therefore, though musically it is excellent for the voice to exploit its complete range, from a practical viewpoint we should use the 'comfortable' zone more than any other, and venture into extreme ranges only rarely, and then only when it is very much to the point.

Finally, we would stress that in vocal music we should concentrate on creating musical values. An audience listens to music, not to words (in fact, especially in choral music, the words are frequently indistinguishable, or so difficult to grasp that listeners ignore them). So the success of vocal music lies largely in its melodic and harmonic qualities, coupled with a convincing musical form. If these factors are good, the words can surely look after themselves. Above all, do not compose word-by-word or line-by-line. Look through the whole text, feel its atmosphere, decide how it can be shaped into a musical form, and then concentrate on the music, and especially on the melody.

7 Accompaniments

The role of accompaniment can vary considerably. Sometimes its importance is minimal, and it must then be unobtrusive, in fact hardly noticed at all. With some kinds of solo song, or even operatic aria, the accompaniment should be a mere background murmur. In other circumstances it may be a very vital part of the whole, sometimes subservient, sometimes stepping forward into complete prominence. Between these two extremes there are obviously many degrees of importance, so we can hardly make hard and fast rules which suit all occasions. We can only generalize, and leave the composer to adapt the ideas put forward here to his own needs.

Taking accompaniment to be in general music of a supporting nature, it has two main roles: to provide atmosphere; and to complete the essence of the music. To take the latter role first, some music needs no accompaniment. Gregorian chant, for instance, is complete without the addition of harmony, and the absence of a metrical pulse obviates the need also for added rhythmic sounds. Other music needs harmonic accompaniment in varying degrees. Often enough, themes need little extra harmonic support, but sometimes without harmonies the melody would sound odd, or not have those rich suggestive qualities which harmonization completes. For example, a modulating theme may sound nonsensical without other notes which guide the harmonic flow. But even in less extreme cases, themes can be greatly enriched by additional harmonies, particularly by a moving bass line which can transform the significance of the rest. For example, the theme of Elgar's *Enigma Variations* is greatly enhanced by the stepwise movement of the bass (see Example 56), and Purcell's great lament from *Dido and Aeneas* would be robbed of much of its eloquence if the chromatically descending bass were omitted.

Accompanying harmonies, with a significant bass, can say much on their own with very little movement. In other cases, where rhythmic pulse is an important component of the accompaniment, the harmonic and rhythmic movements have to be fused together, so that one gives point to the other.

Rhythmic pulse can be a very prominent and essential feature of the music. Without it, much of the significance would disappear (see over, Example 51). At other times it must be subdued and remain a secondary feature. In Example 52 the quaver movement looks restless, but it should be subdued so as to be less an addition to the rhythmic movement than an almost intangible filling-out of the harmonies.

Example 51: Schubert: *Marche Militaire in D*

Example 52: Beethoven: *Sonate Pathétique*, 2nd movt. (adapted)

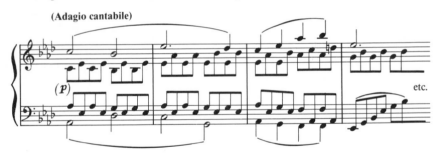

But accompaniment is often much more than a mere 'filling-out'. It can set the real mood of a piece, giving an intimate and unique atmosphere which is a vital part of the essence of the music. Accompaniment is like the background to a painting — it sets the mood of the whole. If a painter wishes to paint a sombre portrait, he first covers the canvas entirely with a dull brown colour. Then, on this background, he paints the portrait and adds a setting which may be indeterminate shades, or room details, or even a landscape. But whatever colours he uses, the sombre brown asserts its tone and the sad atmosphere prevails. On the other hand, if he wants a brilliant, vibrant scene he begins with a bright background, like Van Gogh's southern landscapes. Accompaniment is like this permeating background tone, creating the mood, influencing all that is added to it. In Example 53 Debussy wished to depict footsteps in the snow (the title of the prelude) crossing a sad frozen landscape:

Example 53: Debussy: *Des pas sur la neige* (Préludes, I, 6)

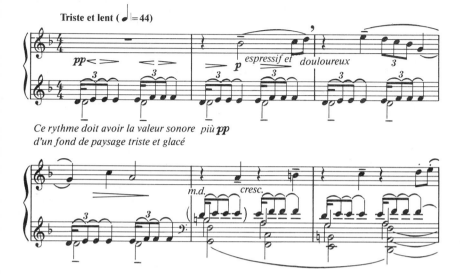

Ce rythme doit avoir la valeur sonore *più pp*
d'un fond de paysage triste et glacé

The composer comments at the beginning: 'this rhythm should create a sound picture of a sad and frozen landscape'. He creates his mood with two factors: harmony and rhythm. The harmony tends to be bare and cold, with an absence of the lushness Debussy generally loved to create. The rhythmic movement of the first bar, with its repetitious, almost tired regularity, represents the heaviness of movement through the deep snow. This rhythm recurs in almost every bar of the piece. It not only creates mood, it is also the chief unifying factor of the music, which otherwise is somewhat fragmentary.

After these preliminary remarks, we will now set out the main methods of accompaniment structure, bearing in mind that frequently one kind of structure may be fused with another, that colour factors may be combined with movement elements, etc.

Doubling the melody with harmonization

In many cases the accompaniment may be no more than a doubling of the melody (at the unison or octave, or even in the bass) with added chordal harmony. This is particularly suited to simple, straightforward music (hymn-tunes, folk-songs, etc.) where no special atmosphere needs to be evoked, or where the composer deliberately wishes to suggest simplicity. In Example 54, from Britten's opera *Peter Grimes*, the first music sung by Ellen Orford has a doubling accompaniment deliberately designed to suggest the character's sin-

61

cerity and purity. The harmony, with its touch of modality, the monochrome orchestration, and the hint of 'organum' parallelisms, add to the almost monastic austerity evoked:

Example 54: Britten: *Peter Grimes*

Naturally, in other accompaniments formed by harmonized doubling, the harmony and orchestration can be made to create other atmospheres — colourful, lush and rich, or harsh and cold, according to the tone colours used and the quality of the harmony.

Doubling of the melody can also be used in accompaniments of a different kind, where all other parts are independent of the theme and unite to form a separate entity. This kind of melodic doubling often occurred in old operas, as if the composer felt the voice needed support. However, today such doubling is seldom used, for several reasons. First, the voice should not need to be helped. Then, singers like to introduce their own free interpretations and cannot possibly coincide with the more precise playing of orchestral instrumentalists or pianists. (Classical singers can be very free in their timing, while those who interpret lighter music are even more so.) Finally, instrumental doubling can impoverish the tone of a singer, especially if the instruments used have thin tone, such as the oboe or upper strings. Nor does piano tone help to fill out the voice. We have written here of doubling vocal melodies, but the same is true if the main protagonist is an instrumentalist, as in a concerto. He is best left alone, and needs neither help nor interference from other players.

Harmonic colour: static

Accompaniment can sometimes be reduced to a very simple harmonic background with very little movement. In Britten's *War Requiem* the tenor solo 'It seemed that out of battle I escaped' (see Example 91) is accompanied by an unchanging sustained G minor chord, indicated to be played 'coldly'. The chord-colour is changed occasionally, and conflicting chords are superimposed momentarily at infrequent points. The tenor often keeps well distant from G minor, and the tonal conflicts created are full of stress. The effect is one of intense strain and desolation, yet the means used are starkly simple.

Static or slow-moving harmonies can be very beautiful as a background for freely ranging melodies, and can be warm or cold according to the harmony and tone-colour used. A sense of movement may be given by scoring for an instrument such as the harp or celesta which can play scales or arpeggios against the static background. Example 55 shows the celesta repeating cascades of sound against sustained semitone clusters in two registers (p. 64). Another simple way of giving a sense of life, even excitement, to static chords is the string tremolo (either bowed tremolo or finger tremolo between two notes) such as begins the Finale of Stravinsky's *Firebird Suite*. Note how in this case the tremolo creates an expectation of the forcefulness and dynamism which is to follow.

Harmonic colour in movement

Commonly enough, melodies are accompanied by harmonies which create atmospheric colour, not through any specific movement of parts (i.e. rhythmic designs) but through the beauty of the harmonies themselves and their special relationship with the melody. In Example 56 the harmonies have a beautiful affinity with the melody; they are so simple, and so absolutely right, that they seem predestined and inevitable. Nothing could be improved. To alter a detail would be to spoil everything.

Example 55: Bartók: *Music for Strings, Percussion and Celesta*

Example 56: Elgar: *Enigma Variations*, Op. 36

This quality of inevitability and rightness should be our aim in harmonizations, and we should cultivate simplicity and directness rather than fussiness and complexity. Avoid too-frequent harmonic change for its own sake. The music in the above example has breadth and serenity because harmonic change is restricted to only two chords a bar. More frequent change would have produced a counterproductive restlessness. In general, frequent harmonic change is best reserved for points of culmination and intensity, or for music of an agitated nature.

Accompaniment based on rhythms

Harmonic colour can well be associated with rhythms which themselves create the atmosphere of a piece. We have already seen this in Debussy's 'Footsteps in the Snow' (Example 53), where a simple two-note rhythmic cell recurs almost throughout the piece. Britten is a master at creating vivid accompaniment figurations which give us a strong impression of the music's emotive message even before the melody begins. Example 57 gives the beginning of one of his *Seven Sonnets of Michelangelo*:

Example 57: Britten: *Seven Sonnets of Michelangelo*

The atmosphere of amorous agitation is instantly created, and is held, unbroken, for most of the piece. Students often hesitate to let a rhythmic design run on for a long period, fearing monotony; they therefore begin something different every few bars, sometimes in the belief that changing words need a constantly changing accompaniment. This is not so. The accompaniment must paint the general background mood of the piece, and rhythmic designs can persist over big areas and only break off if there is a very definite change of mood or subject matter. Admittedly a change can be beneficial, for it gives relief, but it need only be a brief suspension of the general accompanimental rhythmic pattern. In the *Sonnet* just quoted, Britten breaks off the rhythm only near the end, with a few sustained chords, before taking it up again to come to a strong conclusion.

So far we have shown only accompaniment based on a single rhythm. More often, two or more rhythms are used to give not only a more varied rhythmic interest but also a bigger canvas by using first one rhythm, then another, or by using them in various combinations and expansions. Example 58, from Handel's *Messiah*, is an early but outstanding example of a powerful accompaniment based on three rhythmic elements:

Example 58: Handel: *Messiah*, 'Thou shalt break them'

Two elements only are used at first, the 'chord' rhythm of the upbeat quaver chord at the end of each bar, with its resolution on the first beat of the next bar, and then the higher quaver and semiquaver rhythm. These combine well, the chords marching down aggressively and the upper part pointedly expressing energy and spirit. Finally, the third rhythm forms a contrastingly smooth arpeggio which sweeps upwards in pairs of quavers. This arpeggio is used only five times in the whole piece, just enough to relieve the repetitiousness of the other two rhythms. Obviously, without the interruption and relief of the contrasting arpeggio, the accompaniment could never have kept its mordant vitality fresh. Instead it retains its relentless, forceful spirit — an ideal background to the tenor aria which sings of the breaking of the Lord's enemies with a rod of iron, dashing them to pieces like a potter's vessel.

Motifs

Composers have sometimes used a recurring motif or melodic phrase to establish the atmosphere of a piece. This may or may not be joined with the rhythmic designs described in the previous section. A well-known example is the motif in Schubert's *Erlkönig*, which combines perfectly with the dashing octave triplets to conjure up a picture of the father's wild gallop, with his dying son in his arms:

Example 59: Schubert: *Erlkönig*, Op. 1

Ex. 59: (*cont.*)

rei - tet so spät durch Nacht und Wind?

   Motifs can also be used in a more extended way, to unify a long composition which, like opera, moves through many moods and situations. Motifs can be transformed or extended, to say different things, and then perhaps to recall feelings previously evoked. In this way the work retains its unity but can have a wide diversity of atmosphere. We must beware of using an excessive number of motifs. This makes the music less coherent, even enigmatic.

   It is important to emphasize that accompaniments based on motifs or, as in the previous section, on brief rhythmic cells, cannot be successful unless they are formed from well-sculptured, distinctive material. This does not mean they should be complex — indeed complexity can be perplexing and therefore counterproductive. Simple material can be unmistakably right if it has an appropriate urge and impulse. Britten's accompaniments have figured largely in our discussion. They repay study, for he was a master at making brilliant accompaniments out of apparently banal material, and at exploiting little instrumental idiosyncracies to make big background canvases. And every accompaniment he wrote was different. This can hardly be said for composers such as Webern, whose fifty-odd songs have accompaniments which are almost undistinguishable one from another and are certainly unmemorable.

Ostinatos

Ostinatos occur as a brief recurring motif or as a repeating bass in the form of a chaconne or ground. Short repeating ostinatos can be very efficient in creating widely varying atmospheres according to whether they are placid and regularly moving or agitated, with an irregular rhythmic shape. The Berceuse in Stravinsky's *Firebird* has a one-bar ostinato which creates a beautifully tender atmosphere throughout. The actual notes used are not completely constant, as they have to change for tonal reasons, but one has a general impression of constancy through the unchanging regular movement and similarity in note shapes:

Example 60: Stravinsky: Berceuse from *The Firebird*

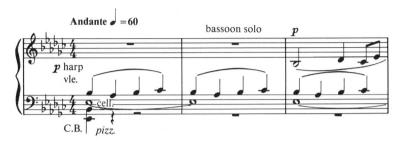

Ostinatos of the chaconne type are usually longer themes of eight, twelve, or even sixteen bars. Though they were much used in Baroque times for aria accompaniment, they have largely fallen out of use, and as the chaconne construction is an art and study in itself we can make no more than a passing mention here. In any case, this type of ostinato is not so much 'atmospheric' accompaniment as the basis of large-scale constructions.

Contrapuntal constructions

Counterpoint of the fugato or canonic type was used as accompaniment in Baroque times, but has now largely fallen out of use, as it fails to express individual mood or atmosphere. However, composers such as Webern have used accompaniments based on canon or loose forms of imitation in both solo and choral pieces. The writing tends to be thin and angular, with little harmonic substance. In Example 61, from Dallapiccola's *Cinque canti*, the accompaniment is formed of metrical canons based on the proportions 1:1:2 and the retrograde 2:1:1, with various basic duration values:

Example 61: Dallapiccola: *Cinque canti*

Though the words are fervent, the accompaniment has an aloof, abstract quality which does little to create a defined background atmosphere. This negative quality is the result of the composer's preference for cerebral concepts over emotive ones — a general attitude in post-war writers.

It is surprising how a similar kind of construction in Bach has an altogether more poetic result. Many of his choral preludes have accompaniments based on rhythmic cells or brief motifs in contrapuntal style, which are expressive of the message of the chorale. In the following accompaniment the main body of the music is formed by cells comprising one long and two short notes, and its retrograde (the same concept as Dallapiccola). It is not easy to decide why the Bach is so much more expressive. Perhaps it is because the parts have rhythmic cohesion and add up to profound harmony — both factors being absent or vague in the Dallapiccola:

Example 62: Bach: *Christ ist erstanden,* Vers. 1

Ex. 62: (cont.)

Percussion

While both tuned and untuned percussion instruments can be used in many
of the forms of accompaniment already mentioned, as part of an ensemble or
orchestra, those of indefinite pitch such as cymbals, gongs, and drums need
special mention because they can be used alone, without using other conventional instruments. As they create sounds with no tonal implications, they
can create fascinating atmospheres which have rich colour but no harmony,
on which voices (sung or spoken) can easily be superimposed. Percussion
instruments of indefinite pitch are of great variety — many different drums,
idiophones of metal, glass, or wood, played by striking, shaking, stroking, or
scraping. The effects are widely varied and can be static shimmers of colour,
rolls comprising crescendos and diminuendos, or simply beaten rhythms,
which can be as complex or simple as one could wish. There is a mystery in
many percussion sounds which can hardly be matched by the whole orchestra. The majesty of a large gong is unique, while a throbbing roll on a big bass
drum can be so quiet that it can be felt rather than be heard, inducing a sense
of the supernatural. Inevitably, composers have been quick to exploit percussion possibilities, and if anything we have suffered a period of over-use. So we
must warn that percussion can easily be overworked and become tiresome. It
is best therefore to err on the quiet side and to use percussion sparingly rather
than to excess. The effect will be all the more telling.

Finally, we have hardly mentioned many conventional accompanimental
ideas which have been used thousands of times and have been invaluable in
their time. The Chopinesque left-hand arpeggios, the repeated chords of
Mozart and Beethoven, Strauss's waltz rhythms, popular song accompaniments (with bass on the downbeats, chords on the upbeats), and so on — all
are already so familiar to us that it has seemed superfluous and pedantic to
describe them. If a student wishes to use them, by all means let him do so
without hesitation. However, it has been our aspiration to introduce ideas of
more novelty and distinction, urging students to write accompaniments
which have originality and may provide a unique framework for the melody
and words which express the composer's more intimate feelings.

8 The piece as a whole

Melody and accompaniment

So far, melody and accompaniment have been treated separately. This is because it is essential to have a good command of both before trying to combine them. Unfortunately, many students begin a piece by trying to think of melody and accompaniment together, and after a few bars can go no further. It is simply impossible, especially for a beginner, to put down the whole of the music bar by bar, beat by beat.

Whatever kind of music we are writing, we must move forward with the most essential factor (usually melody) for at least an adequate distance before turning back to consider the rest. Even at this stage it is preferable only to sketch in secondary details, fragmentary accompaniment ideas, etc., before completing a whole section of the main subject matter. In this way, a good part of the form of the entire piece is well determined. We can either go on, or turn back to fill in the secondary material or accompaniment.

This is not to say that the general design of the accompaniment cannot be conceived right from the start, as a fairly well-defined mental image. This may be an advantage, as with the accompaniment design in mind the melody will probably be more appropriately shaped. We could also decide on points where the accompaniment could take over for a brief period, or perhaps form a dialogue with the melody. However, it must remain a background thought in our minds and not be an obstacle to our concentration on the melodic creation.

As the melody goes forward we can pencil in occasional ideas for harmony, the bass progression, perhaps a detail of movement in some inner part. But these details must be no more than reminders, ideas which can later be used or rejected. To make supporting details too precise at this stage would be wrong, because they may need to be undone later on. It is better to attack the whole question of accompaniment when we have an entire melodic section complete. Then we can look at it in its entirety, see the whole problem, and shape harmonies, rhythmic details, form, texture, etc., into the best possible mould.

Introductions and interludes

Often enough, an instrumental or vocal piece begins with an introduction. It is best not to attempt to write this until the rest of the piece is fairly complete. Instead, most students begin with an introduction which is absolutely irrelevant, has nothing to do with what follows, and is never heard of again. The introduction must use material from the main body of the music — sometimes it will quote from the main melody, sometimes begin with the accompaniment figure itself, or the two may be combined. The essential point is that the introduction prepares for what is to come, and is a unified part of it.

The same is true of interludes: they must be associated with the rest of the music. But we must be aware that often enough interludes have a special purpose. They may serve as very essential periods of repose, or provide a contrast in mood. If a piece of music is frenetic and forceful, it may well be that an interlude is a peaceful moment like the 'calm before the storm'. On the other hand, a generally ponderously sombre piece may need stimulating by interludes of contrastingly more vital movement. But whatever the circumstances, through our technical resources we can use some element of the main music and adapt it to serve our purpose, so that unity is preserved.

Very occasionally it is good to have interludes of completely new material as long as the mood is right and a satisfactory form created. For instance, one could have a form in which special interludes have a natural place such as:

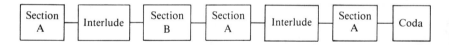

There are of course many variants of such schemes, suitable for use in single-movement works of 20-minute duration down to short movements of only a few minutes. Inevitably, the interlude material should not have the strength of character of the main section material. It should hold us in suspense and give us a sense of waiting and expectation for the more important message which is to follow.

Instrumentation

How can we write for instruments if we know nothing about them? I have seen all too many student pieces which betray, in every bar, ignorance of how instruments work and what they can do. The only way to write well for an instrument and exploit its full potentials is to know it intimately well. But how can one do this with so many instruments?

There are two solutions: one is to devour a treatise on instruments, instrumentation, and orchestration; the other is to learn to play enough instruments so that we can learn the main performing principles of each of the main instrumental groups — strings, woodwind, brass, and keyboard. After this, we must observe constantly what happens in the orchestra. What is the relative balance of instruments? What is the effect of their different registers and tone-colours? How do they combine?

I think it is much more valuable to hear and play instruments than to read about them. As we write for an instrument we must be playing it in our imagination, with the right bowings and fingerings, feeling the sensations of different registers, expressing ourselves through the different tones and timbres, the possibilities of legato, staccato, vibrato, etc.

Admittedly, we have no time to learn every instrument, but it is certainly possible to get to know the workings of one each of the string, woodwind, and brass groups. From these we can deduce the rest. My own method was to learn the piano, clarinet, and saxophone early on, and then (helped by a pawnbroker) investigate almost every orchestral instrument. My brother gave me his guitar, and I inherited a violin, which I learned well. Then I took up the double bass and organ for good measure. My chief tutor was *Harmsworth's Self Educator.* Orchestration I learned by copying gramophone records.

I don't recommend this multi-instrumental method for everyone. There is a danger that we neglect a profound study of a main instrument, and end up as mediocrities. However, we do gain a wide knowledge of what is needed in composition and orchestration.

As this is not an instrumentation treatise we must go no further on the subject, except to repeat that notes must not be written in the abstract. We must write them as if we were playing, grouping certain notes in slurs, with staccato, legato, and sforzando, the rise and fall of each phrase marked with crescendo and diminuendo, etc. Music without slurs and dynamics looks dead, because it has not been brought to life. But to be able to include these indications intelligently and with musicianship we must be able to play in our minds.

9 Choral music

Though the musical world seems to be divided between the slightly opposing camps of instrumentalists and choralists, nobody can deny that choral music — with or without accompaniment — can be a very powerful, colourful, and attractive means of expression. And it is often at its most powerful and poetic when it is simple and direct — indeed, excessive complexity takes away from its effectiveness. Choral music is therefore a good starting point for beginners in composition, and not infrequently we find quite effective works written for choir at an early stage of development.

The principles of effective choral writing are fairly straightforward, and mostly comprise exploitation of the choir's colouristic resources in what can be called 'choral orchestration', coupled with simple variation in the density of voices and a limited use of contrapuntal effects. Today, it would be unusual to write in the Renaissance madrigal manner, or the *fugato* style of the Baroque era. (One conspicuous exception is the four-part canon in the *Caritas* section of Stravinsky's *Canticum sacrum* — not a musical episode of great universal appeal.) Modern choral forms tend to avoid idioms so closely associated with past epochs, and ideally each piece should have its own particular form, which is a compromise between the form of the words and the needs of the music. The music, to be satisfactory, may need contrasting sections, differing textures, and periods of thematic recall; and such factors must not only be compatible with the text, but should also form a whole which is a perfect expression of the words.

If the words are subdivided into similar verses the musical solution may be quite simple, but when this is not so an ideal musical form may not be easy to find. As we have said, each piece will have its own form, so no set patterns or rules can be formulated. All we can say is that logical, easily perceptible solutions are always preferable to enigmatic ones, which may have forms so difficult to perceive that to the listener they seem formless.

The words

Choral music is best suited to simple, lyrical texts where nothing is superfluous. In fact, too few words are far preferable to too many. If we want to paint a big choral canvas, words can be repeated without any fear of being repetitious, or we can use whole sentences or sections several times over. This kind of repetition serves to consolidate the main message of the text (which may otherwise not be sufficiently evident), and can also conveniently serve the ends (through musical restatement) of giving a strong, coherent musical form.

Words in narrative form are hardly suited to choral use, though they can occasionally find their place in some kind of chanting, or may be spoken by a narrator or part of a choir. In fact, a very good means of creating a contrasting episode is to have narration against a quiet, sustained choral background. However, this suits the ethos only of certain 'modern' works, and in less contemporary idioms is normally avoided.

To sum up, when looking for a choral text, choose words which are simple, direct, and poetic. If the text is too short, consider the possibility of repetition.

Bear in mind that choral music tends to obscure the clarity of words, and that at a first hearing few people will understand them, their attention inevitably being concentrated on the music. The situation is far worse if we use Latin or another foreign language. The text may of course be printed in the programme, but this is by no means a common usage. Since we cannot count on people grasping much of the words at a first hearing it is the musical qualities which will contribute to the success or failure of a choral piece. Of course titles are important, for they can influence our emotions and prepare our moods before we hear a note. 'Music, when soft voices die' begins to move our hearts long before the music even begins.

Choral textures

There are many ways of writing for choir, some simple, some complex. There are at least ten or a dozen different principal textures, but it would be unusual to find a large number of them used in the same piece. One of their main purposes is to effect change and relief from the monotony of a single texture, but excessive change will lead to confusion. One must therefore use the various possibilities with restraint and purpose, putting a limit on the variety of textures used.

The following possibilities of choral orchestration are limited to the most-used textures; traditional forms such as fugato, fugue, and canon are omitted, being too closely identified stylistically with past epochs to be of effective use today (though some mention of them will be made later).

Homophony

One of the most effective and simple choral textures is homophony, in which all parts move together, melody with harmony. Homophony is probably the commonest choral texture of all, and has been used in all periods. It is very effective in quiet passages where the beauty of melody and harmony are undisturbed by counterpoint, as in Example 63, from Messiaen's *O Sacrum convivium*: [1]

Example 63: Messiaen: *O sacrum convivium*

The effect here is tranquil and smooth, yet homophony may also give the best texture for decisive, dynamic expressions. As all the voices hammer out the same syllables together, the accentuation is at its sharpest (Example 64, overleaf).

Homophony with independent movement

True homophony — where all parts move exactly together — can become monotonous and inflexible, so composers frequently introduce a little independent movement among the voice parts (Example 65).

[1] In order to save space, choral examples are here written on only two staves. Instead, choral music should have one stave for each voice, though divided parts can be written together on one line. Tenor parts should be written using the treble clef with an '8' attached to the tail, signifying that the sound is to be an octave lower than it is written. In other words, tenor parts should be written an octave above the real sounds.

Example 64: Walton: *Belshazzar's Feast*

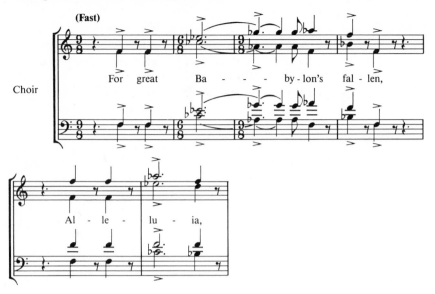

Choir

Example 65: Dowland: *Now, O Now, I Needs Must Part*

Up to this point, Dowland's piece has been almost exclusively homophonic, but in the last four beats of the third bar quoted above the voices each have slight differences in note-lengths and the placing of syllables. This gives an illusion of a richer polyphonic texture and relieves the sameness of homophony. It is often sufficient to break the homophony in one voice only to give this added touch of interest.

Unfortunately, students' work in this texture tends towards excessive breaking-up of the homophonic movement. Each part is so busy with different rhythmic movements that the simple directness of homophony is lost. The result is music which is overloaded with restless movement of little significance. Simplicity is preferable to ineffectual obscurity.

Monophony

Strictly speaking, monophonic music is a single melodic line, without harmony or even octaves. But in choral music we can include music under this term which is either at the unison or in octaves. If all the voices sing in unison, the sopranos have to sing rather low and the basses too high, so unison singing of the whole choir is seldom used. However, in quiet passages it can be most effective and the balance of the voices good. The use of monophony in octaves is much more frequent, and is in fact an excellent contrast to homophony (Example 66):

Example 66: Finzi: *My spirit sang all day*

Here, the first phrase in octaves is highly dynamic, but the sudden burst of harmony in the second bar has a strength and vitality which goes beyond what could have been achieved in octaves; the effect is striking. Note how the highest (and loudest) notes are kept in reserve for this decisive bar.

Pairing

In the third bar of Example 66, Finzi changes the texture yet again, to 'pairing'. The two upper parts and two lower ones separate and finally join together only at the words 'could say'. This separation of the two pairs of voices is achieved by using longer 'holding notes'. While one pair moves, the other holds sustained notes; then the procedure is reversed. This brief pairing of parts in a loose form of imitation or counterpoint is best done by pairing the women's voices as one unit and the men's voices as the other. This gives better tonal contrast than any other pairing. However, octave pairing between soprano and tenor or alto and bass comes off well and can give a powerful melodic line, as Example 67 shows. Here the harmony is complete, yet the melody is quite dominant. Note how the melody is kept in a high register (for power), while the less important accompanying parts are in a lower, more subdued range.

Example 68, a setting of a carol by Kodály, shows a resourceful use of octave pairing in the upper parts and close imitation by the men's voices in thirds. This music is simplicity itself, yet the skilful use of pairings and imitation yields a vital expression which has both subtlety and intellectual appeal.

Solo and accompaniment

Though the sound of solo voice with choral accompaniment can be very beautiful, composers have largely failed to exploit this resource, possibly because they are well aware that a good solo voice may not always be available. However, occasional use has been made of groups of voices (e.g. all the sopranos) singing together, supported by a quiet background of the other parts. In such 'solo' or 'quasi solo' passages, the accompaniment is best kept very simple, so as not to divert attention from the melody. The accompaniment sounds very well when it is hummed, with perhaps a few words here and

Example 67: Chávez: *Tree of Sorrow*

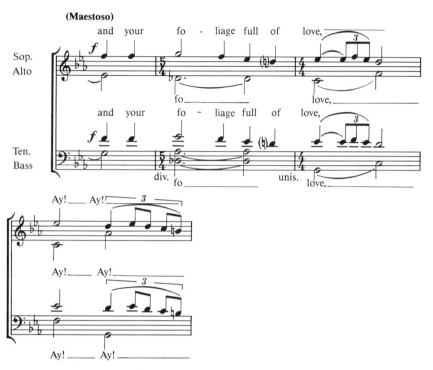

Example 68: Kodály: *A Christmas Carol*

there while the solo part rests, or to join with it at a point of culmination. One can often choose just a few significant words for the accompaniment, and avoid the rest. For example, in a piece such as 'Swing low, sweet chariot' the accompaniment could use only the words 'Swing low', and just here and there (and especially at the end) join the soloist at the repeated 'coming for to carry me home'. Example 69 is a simple example of sopranos singing 'solo' while other voices hum a quiet chordal background:

Example 69: Spiritual: *I've been in the storm*

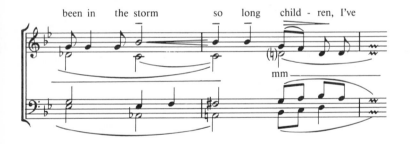

Two or more layers

Choral writing similar to solo and accompaniment can divide the music into two strata, or layers, as Example 70 from my own work *Discoveries* shows. The lower voices have here more significance than mere accompaniment. They have harmonic and melodic qualities which make them complete in themselves, yet they work together as a separate layer, in a kind of dialogue with the soprano melody. This kind of 'layering' is most effective in producing a texture which is more interesting than homophony, yet is still very clear and simple. It is of course important that the 'accompanying' layer does not have its clarity and identity confused by too much individual voice movement.

Example 70: Smith Brindle: *Discoveries*

This layering principle can be extended so that there are several voices in each layer. For example, one could write for six-part choir and have three upper and three lower voices in two separate strata, or use a nine-part choir, three different layers of three voices each, etc. Carl Orff uses such multi-voiced layering to excellent effect, yet retains great simplicity, clarity, and directness.

From here it is only a short step to polychoral music — two or more choirs separately positioned. However, as this is not a treatise on the Venetian tradition, we will leave the subject here, with no more than a reminder of its possibilities.

Ostinatos

In multi-layered music, one or more layer can be an ostinato (a repeated phrase which creates the background atmosphere of a piece and gives it unity and cohesion). In Example 71 the two lower voices have 'clanging' motifs which evoke the atmosphere of the blacksmith's forge:

Example 71: Kodály: *God's Blacksmith*

Here the ostinatos are unchanging pedal notes, but of course they could be recurring musical designs with changing harmonic potential to give them both a structural and an emotional purpose.

Counterpoint

We have already said how modern choral music tends to avoid a recall of Renaissance or Baroque atmospheres by abandoning the use of choral writing typical of these epochs – fugato, fugue, canon, and other contrapuntal constructions. For example, *fugato* is so closely associated with the old oratorio style that it would be difficult to use this contrapuntal technique at all without evoking such an atmosphere. However, some modern composers have deliberately wished to recall the past — Stravinsky wrote a double fugue as the slow movement of his *Symphony of Psalms,* while the other movements recall Medieval and Renaissance styles. A too-obvious recall of the past is avoided by two factors: the degree of dissonance used, and the character of the orchestral accompaniment. For instance, though some choral sections of Stravinsky's first movement are almost like Medieval plainchant, the atmosphere of the music is dominated by the motor rhythm of the slightly dissonant accompaniment, with its cross-rhythms and dynamic pulsations giving a modern, machine-like character.

Quite an amount of modern choral music similarly uses old choral textures, while an effect of 'modernity' is produced through giving the harmony an unusual degree of dissonance for such choral styles. It is surprising how much 20th-century choral music is based on textures of the early Renaissance, yet this fact has almost passed unnoticed. Such widely varied writers as Webern, Dallapiccola, and Stravinsky rely heavily on the textures and idioms of early choral music. The note patternings are really very simple in rhythmic outline, very closely resembling those of early choral music. The big difference lies in the degree of chromaticism and dissonance used and the often widely-leaping intervals. Example 72, from Webern's *Das Augenlicht*, is very close indeed to Renaissance canonic writing from a rhythmic standpoint, but of course the large leaps and harsh dissonances give a sound which is quite untypical of that period (see next page). Admittedly, much modern choral music using early music textures is of a religious nature, but not all, and *Das Augenlicht* is an obvious exception.

Number of voices

Because students are usually taught four-part harmony, and there are four conventional voices (soprano, alto, tenor, and bass), they tend always to write for the conventional four-part mixed choir, thus ignoring the existence of the most common voices of all (mezzo soprano and baritone). They also avoid the division of parts, as if it were something of extreme difficulty, and forget altogether that it is by no means necessary to have all the voices singing all the

Example 72: Webern: *Das Augenlicht*

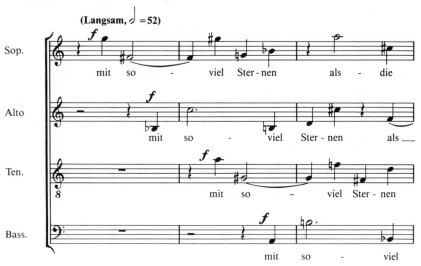

time. However, it must be admitted that many of the greatest choral composers also restricted their horizons in very much the same way.

In fact, choral music can be very flexible as to the number of parts. Any voice can be divided easily into two or even three separate parts, and we need have no fear that listeners will easily detect that some voices have been correspondingly weakened. On the contrary, multiplicity of parts gives an impression of strength and fullness, so if anything division of parts produces added strength rather than a weakening. In any case, choral singers tend to apply themselves more strongly when divided parts create in them a sense of greater responsibility and individuality.

Effects

Over the last twenty-five years the choral vocabulary has been considerably expanded to explore many sound effects never conventionally used before.

Tone clusters are created by voices singing at various pitches around certain zones (medium, low, or high) or around certain notes. Each singer chooses his or her own particular pitch. This gives a beautiful sound which can be mysteriously elusive or vividly powerful. At the same time, other voices may sing conventionally or add various other effects.

It has become more usual to use a speaking choir, either with all voices together, or in different parts, or with each voice speaking quite independently. Alternatively, a single voice can narrate in speech while the choir sings a sustained background. In this way, one can use a narrative text which would otherwise be too wordy for normal choral usage.

Whispering is most effective, with the voices either all together or in various parts. The dynamic level is quite low, so it makes a good background to a spoken narration or a solo singer.

In addition, all kinds of noises can be exploited — clapping, breathing sounds, chest-beating, and so on. Also, any effect or unconventional usage can be combined with others or with singing. We have also the possibility of electronic amplification and distortion. All this gives a new palette of sounds and colours which can be exploited to give vivid and poetic new sensations. All one needs is imagination.

Unfortunately, effects tend to wear out and to become over familiar. For this reason they are bound to remain as very secondary aids to choral music, which to be genuinely original and vital needs musicianship much more than exploitation of mere sound effects.

10 Technical expansions: 1

Many students feel the urge to get away from conventional musical idioms. Indeed, in this stereotyped world many of us have a longing to do something which is artistically original, in some way to leave our mark on the musical scene. Indeed, if we leave only the slightest sign of our passing we should be satisfied. This desire to be different is part of the psychological formation of some composers, and motivates their desire to create. However, it should not be the only reason for their creative activity, which should rather stem from less egotistic desires.

Putting aside these perhaps superfluous thoughts, it is nevertheless evident that from the beginning some students prefer to write 'differently' but lack the technical resources to do so competently. Their work is obviously the result of struggle, of trying to create something coherent without knowing exactly what that something is, or how to find it. This part of the book deals with possibilities, moving gradually further away from conventionalities, so that step by step the student can absorb and use more and more unusual idioms. Then, given these foundation techniques, he can go on and perhaps invent his own idiom and fulfil his ideals.

However, we will have to cover a great deal of territory in a limited space if the cost of this book is not to become prohibitive. So I beg to be forgiven beforehand if new possibilities and technical expansions are only outlined, and not investigated at length. Also, I believe most students prefer to be introduced to new ideas which they can explore for themselves with a sense of adventure, rather than be led on a Cook's Tour with every fact and statistic recited. A student's intuition moves far more swiftly than can an instruction manual, and I believe that self-tuition is the finest form of education. In any case, it could well be that some students have no interest at all in certain idioms and prefer to by-pass them quickly in their search for what expresses their own aesthetic more closely.

We will be dealing here mostly with the simple techniques of putting notes together in certain special ways, but in reality this is only part of the story. Complete 'idioms' are the fusion of musical techniques with other factors — aesthetic, social, even political — which have influenced composers and stimulated them to mould their music into certain well-defined styles. We can by no means consider here such a wide range of factors, and it is essential that students supplement this reading with other books of a historical and analytical nature to complete the picture. Nevertheless, the study we propose will give a good foundation for exploration, and is certainly the most essential and important investigation of all for the young composer who wants to find his way ahead.

Free pentatonic music

Pentatonic scales (scales of five notes) have been used since the pyramids were built (according to archaeological finds and to musicological deductions from pictures of flute, harp, and lute players), and are still used today, in abundance. A great many popular songs use nothing else in their melodies, though they may have triadic harmony in the accompaniment (two 'evergreen' examples are shown below). The paramount feature of pentatonic scales is the absence of semitones:

Example 73

This absence of semitones has two effects: there is no leading note to pull towards the tonic; and no fourth degree note to gravitate down to the third. Being without these tensions, pentatonic tones are therefore more bland, movement between them is free, and there is not such a strong feeling of the need for resolution as in the diatonic system. Secondly, from a harmonic point of view, as it is impossible to form chords such as the dominant with pentatonic scales, the harmony is slightly static, there being no decisive reso-

lution or strong cadences. This can create a beautifully smooth harmony with
a feeling of noble purity:

Example 74: Debussy: *Voiles* (Préludes, I, 2)

In Example 74 many of the harmonies are left incomplete, in that full triad
chords hardly occur. This is typical of pentatonic harmony, which can be
manipulated in many ways to give either an archaic quality or a sense of
modernity. Example 75 illustrates various ways of exploiting this kind of
harmonic versatility:

Example 75a

Example 75b

Example 75c

In (a) the accompaniment is in archaic-sounding fourths and fifths, giving a slight feeling of *organum*. Triads have been deliberately omitted (though they are of course possible) in order to give this timeless, Medieval harmonic feeling. In (b) the same melodic note-succession is accompanied by chords which include a certain number of triads, some with sevenths, others without thirds. This gives a nicely varied harmony, still with an archaic feeling. At (c) the same succession of notes is very differently treated. No triad is included, and there has been a deliberate attempt to contradict conventional harmonic usage and produce a stressful harmonic feeling. Note that bass notes are mostly dissonant with the melody, and that there has been little attempt to remove note-relationships which conventionally would be regarded as crude and unmusical. This shows the use of the pentatonic scale to produce music of a mildly modern flavour, with that element of harmonic stress which contemporary expression often demands.

This kind of idiom is particularly useful where one wishes to include a slightly archaic flavour at some point in a composition which otherwise uses a more contemporary idiom. The 'dissonant pentatonic' idiom is sufficiently non-harmonic to be welded with less tonal situations. It is worth noting that while it would be a gross aesthetic blunder to introduce music of more classical times (from the Baroque onwards) into contemporary music, one can introduce earlier music quite successfully. The aesthetic feeling of the very old is sufficiently near to that of certain contemporary expressions to allow a natural blending.

It is, of course, important not to introduce modulations or key transitions; this would distort the idiom, destroying its essential freedom from tonal harmony with its well-defined key relationships.

Free diatonicism

It is possible to use the diatonic system in several ways to give an air of 'modernity'. We usually tend to discard the diatonic system because the harmonic effect is too plain, 'C-majorish', conventional, and triadic. On the contrary, it can be given a sharp, stressful edge by writing in such a way that the usual triadic structure is partly or totally demolished. In Example 76(a), below, triads are present only below the melody notes D and E, but are contradicted in each case by dissonant sounds. In (b) the triadic system is avoided completely, so that no conventional triads are used or suggested. The harmonic effect is dissonant, but not unpleasantly so, and the absence of chromaticism means that a background feeling of unity typical of the diatonic system is retained:

Example 76a

Example 76b

The conventional diatonic system can be disrupted in many other ways without going into the realms of chromatic harmony, bitonality, polytonality, etc. Composers have often introduced dissonant diatonic notes into otherwise straightforward harmonic situations to give the desired touch of dissonance or unconventionality. At one time this was known as the 'wrong note' technique, favoured by such composers as Stravinsky. Example 77 shows part of the score of his *Symphony of Psalms* (some instrumental parts are omitted for the sake of clarity):

Example 77: Stravinsky: *Symphony of Psalms*

This passage is based on a four-note ostinato: E♭, B♭, F, B♭; as will be seen, the choral parts and ostinato come close to, but never quite reach, conventional triadic usage. In every chord there is some foreign element, some contradiction which gives an odd twist to the harmony. Instead of a feeling of positive harmonic movement from one chord to another, there is a still, static mood of unusual beauty, created by harmonic uncertainty. Note that the four-note ostinato is at odds with the triple metre, so that it can recur only in its original place (at the beginning of a bar) every four bars. The uncertainty of this metrical contradiction also contributes to the static mood.

A further use of free diatonicism is the formation of note clusters in which a number of adjacent notes are played together. This obscures a clear sense of chordal harmony. In soft passages the effect can be quite beautiful, but with loud and harsh tones the dissonances can be very forceful.

Composers sometimes use an attenuated form of this cluster effect to obscure what would otherwise be perfectly normal chord sequences. For instance, Stravinsky's *Symphonies of Wind Instruments* ends with nine bars based on the chord progressions E minor, D minor, and C major, but by adding foreign diatonic notes to each chord he forms small clusters which obscure the harmony and give it a mysterious fascination. Example 78 is a simplified version of these three chords, showing the orchestration:

Example 78: Stravinsky: Final Chords in *Symphonies of Wind Instruments*

Note that the lower notes form tenths, without foreign notes. This gives strength to the harmony. Foreign notes are added higher up: A and D to the chord of E minor; B, E, and C to that of D minor; and B and D to C major. This method of obscuring chords only in higher registers is quite usual, as it gives a gool equilibrium to the harmony. To do otherwise would give a crude, aesthetically poor effect. (Note that in the natural harmonic series the lower notes are the most consonant, while higher up dissonances become more, but not disturbingly, acute. Composers have followed the same pattern.)

A further way of obscuring diatonic chords is by using counter parallelisms, in which every move in the upper part(s) is reflected by inversion in the lower:

Example 79a

Example 79b

In (a) the upper and lower parts are formed of triads with an added note in the upper part. Their contrary motion produces vertical combinations which can be consonant or dissonant, but the result sounds quite logical and smooth. Example (b) shows the same effect using fourth chords instead of triads. The effect is still good, but harmonically more obscure and dissonant. Naturally, one can use such counter-parallelisms in many other ways, using more dissonant-type chords, or a more slender texture. We will return to this concept in a chromatic texture later on.

The whole-tone scale

The whole-tone, or hexatonic, scale comprises only tones and no semitones, and so only two different scales are possible (Example 80):

Example 80

As the mixing of these two scales would introduce semitones and produce an effect of chromaticism, usually, in order to create the particular mood of whole-tone music, only one is used at a time. Furthermore, as scales can begin on any note, and as all notes are equal, there is no 'tonic' and no effect of 'supertonic', 'mediant', etc. Indeed, as the conventional dominant does not exist in a whole-tone scale (perfect fifths are not available), there cannot possibly be effects of resolution such as we find in dominant–tonic harmonic movements. The harmonic effect is therefore without the strong forward movement of diatonic music, and composers have used whole-tone harmony (particularly in the Impressionist period) to give tranquil, passive moods, and delicate colourings:

Example 81: Debussy: *Voiles* (Préludes, I, 2)

A suspended, almost immobile quality is the most obvious characteristic of the whole-tone scale. Note that as far as triad chords are concerned, a whole-tone scale comprises only two different chords, as the notes of a chord on the first degree are repeated in chords on the third and fifth degrees, while those of a chord on the second degree are repeated on the fourth and sixth. In other words, chords on the third to sixth degrees of the scale are only inversions of chords on the first and second degrees:

Example 82

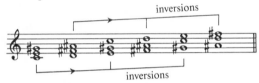

Clearly this makes for rather meagre harmonic material if we limit ourselves only to triadic usage, so it is better to exploit other kinds of chord shapes which will serve to produce impressions of greater harmonic variety. The following shows how chord shapes can be varied considerably to give a more fruitful harmonic language. (The chords shown in Example 83 are limited only to those with the root on C, and are mostly given with notes in close formation. Of course the component notes could be spread over various registers in many ways, giving wide possibilities.):

Example 83

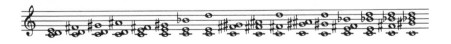

From a melodic point of view, the whole-tone scale has weak features. As all notes are (in theory) the same in melodic strength, and none predominates over the others, the notes do not have a decisive tendency to 'go somewhere'. They tend to be somewhat static, so the contours of phrases can be rather weak.

Worse still, composers tend to keep their melodic designs within scalic patterns, which soon become over-obvious and artificial. (As Example 81 shows, Debussy himself had this scalic tendency.) It is best to hide scale patterns by introducing leaps which not only hide this weakness in the system, but also allow stronger, more memorable phrase contours. In Example 84 the melody essentially rises and falls over an octave, but by introducing upward and downward leaps of thirds and sixths the scale pattern is completely broken up:

Example 84: Smith Brindle: *Canto-Guitarcosmos II*

From a harmonic point of view the whole-tone system is very versatile. As no semitones, major sevenths, minor ninths, etc., are possible, the maximum amount of dissonance obtainable is through either adjacent tones or the more benign tritone. If the dissonance of a tone is avoided, the harmony can sound both rich and smooth:

Example 85

Notice the preponderance of tritones, thirds, and sixths in the above example. Possible dissonances (tones) are well separated, and by becoming sevenths and ninths the strength of conflict is reduced.

In the above, some attempt has been made to produce well-sounding harmony, but the whole-tone system has so little conflict within itself that almost any combination of notes can sound tolerable. The worst effects are produced by:

(1) Chords which have adjacent notes or clusters, in a low register.

(2) Chords with poor equilibrium, e.g. notes close together in a low register and other notes far apart in higher octaves. (When notes are close together in a low register they sound crude and clumsy, and fail to give a good bass to the harmony. Conversely, if notes are far apart their harmonic relationship is weakened and they loose their normal inter-relationship. Thus, the quality of both dissonances and consonances is dissipated by distance.)

(3) Poor horizontal flow through lack of note-change. When notes are repeated in successive chords they lose their power and become weak. If we change notes from chord to chord this weakening does not occur — the notes retain their 'freshness'. However, as there are only six notes in the system it is obvious that in four-part harmony without octave doublings only two notes can remain unused in each chord, and in five-part harmony only one note; in six-part harmony all notes are used in each chord, even though the registers change. One solution could be to double notes at the octave, but this leads to poor results, as doubled notes become too powerful and upset the chordal equilibrium. A better solution is to work as follows: as each chord changes, use as many 'new' notes as are available; if some notes have to be repeated, change their register, and they will lose less of their freshness. This was the system used in Example 85.

The whole-tone system can combine well with other compositional methods, though considerable skill and sensitivity are needed. It can be fused into a highly chromatic technique such as serialism. Example 86 gives the series from Dallapiccola's *Quaderno musicale di Annalibera*, together with a brief musical quotation:

Example 86: Dallapiccola: *Quaderno musicale di Annalibera*

Ex. 86: (cont.)

Series

Notes 4, 5, and 6, and 7, 8, and 9 in the series form two whole-tone groups belonging to different scales, while the first and last three-note groups form two unrelated tonal centres. The two whole-tone groups are used as pivots between such tonal zones throughout the composition, and give the work its precise character. The same device was used by the composer in long works such as the *Canti di liberazione* and the opera *Ulysses*, both serial works with characteristically potent harmony. Clearly he set great store on the value of whole-tone harmony and the versatility of a system which could fuse together tonal zones which would otherwise not easily be compatible.

The whole-tone system can combine well with the archaic modes, giving a gentle harmonic stress which turns the atmosphere more towards the 20th century. In Example 87, an organ piece, the plainsong Kyrie from the *Fons bonitatis* Mass is accompanied by chords from the whole-tone system:

Example 87: Smith Brindle: *Fons bonitatis*

The plainchant is in the Phyrigian mode (with a final on E), so that there is conflict between F, G, A, and B of the plainchant and F♯, G♯, and A♯ in the whole-tone scale. C, D, and E are common to both the mode and the whole-tone system. (It is perhaps worth noting that if the whole-tone scale had been that which begins on D♭ the degree of conflict would have been less.)

Chords based on whole-tones can occur in many other systems, even in diatonic harmony (e.g. the ninth chord G, B, F, A), but of course they sound perfectly in place and not as if they have merely been temporarily extracted from the whole-tone system. Whole-tone harmony is part of many harmonic systems, is valuable in many circumstances, and is therefore worth a brief study by all composers, even if they have no intention of using it as a complete system themselves.

Bitonality and polytonality

The neo-classical period of the 1920s and 1930s had as one of its ideals a return to the past, avoiding Romantic expressions (which were held in contempt) and taking up mainly the styles of the Baroque era. This 'Back to Bach' movement had a substantial problem, however: a too-faithful recreation of Bach or Vivaldi sounds old and dated, as well as probably being inferior to the genuine article. But in spite of returning to old forms, composers wished their music to have that feeling of nervous stress and tension which is so typical of modern art in general. One certain way of making the old forms sound 'modern' was to introduce a greater degree of dissonance and to avoid the euphony of the original conventional harmony. One device introduced to create harmonic stress was that of writing in two or more different keys or modes at the same time − to write bitonal and polytonal music. Even up to the present day some composers still use this conflict of tonalities as one of their technical resources. The effect or mood created can be varied considerably, according to the composer's aesthetic aims, from a mildly piquant flavour, through rough, spiky textures, to sensations of mordant, acrid harshness.

Example 88 is a simple example of music in two keys or modes at the same time:

Example 88: Bartók: 'Harvest Song' from *44 Duos for Two Violins*

Ex. 88: (*cont.*)

Both parts are in the Dorian mode, the upper violin part on D, and the lower on G♯. These modal 'tonalities' are a tritone apart, and are thus in the greatest possible conflict; the result, however, is almost bland. This is because the two parts are mostly consonant with each other, avoiding excessive dissonance. Note that the parts are mostly well separated and do not cross. This enhances the clarity and intelligibility of each part. (Ravel's Sonata for violin and cello has a very similar passage to Bartók's piece, with very similar key characteristics.)

It is worth trying the effect of combining various keys, by choosing a simple subject and experimenting with canons at various distances in various keys. In general, one can say that if closely related keys are chosen (e.g. C and G, or

C and F) the bitonal effect will be minimal, perhaps even unnoticeable. If tonalities are not closely related the tonal conflict will be more evident according to the degree of disagreement between the scales. For example, scales a tritone or a semitone apart have only two notes in common; all other notes are different, and so one can expect a considerable degree of conflict unless (as in the Bartók example) adequate vertical consonance can be maintained. In general it would seem that keys a minor third apart have just the right degree of conflict, and are well suited to this technique. Their scales have three notes in conflict but four in common, so that the balance is weighted slightly in favour of compatibility between the keys, while there is enough stress available when needed.

It must be noted that with this technique modulations are quite unnecessary — in fact they would be pointless and contrary to the spirit of the music. A clear modulation would create an aesthetic feeling foreign to bitonality. In longer pieces composers often use varied keys, so as to have a more chromatic language at their disposal and to avoid the stagnation of using only a limited selection of notes. However, they avoid modulations and leap from one key to another freely and abruptly. Sometimes key changes can be used as formal divisions, as they help to give more definition to the beginning of new sections. For example, in the Bartók piece quoted above there is a moment of rest at mid-point, on the finals of the two modes (D and G♯). After this, the music begins again in new tonalities, with roles reversed and counterpoints inverted. The second violin plays the inverted melody in A, and the first violin the inverted accompaniment in E♭. The piece ends with both instruments in the same key — E♭ minor.

Before leaving bitonality, we would like to quote an example in contrast to the smooth euphony of the Bartók Violin Duo, a euphony achieved despite the considerable conflict of keys. In Example 89, from Stravinsky's *Symphonies of Wind Instruments*, the mood is very different — harsh and bitter, despite the almost carefree jauntiness of the melody:

Example 89: Stravinsky: *Symphonies of Wind Instruments*

Ex. 89: (*cont.*)

The harshness is the result of two opposing factors: the two upper flutes play harmoniously together in G♭; the lowest flute is in G major. But in addition to this harsh semitone difference of keys, Stravinsky has deliberately created strong dissonances between the lower parts, the third flute disagreeing with the second at almost every move.

This example is quoted to underline the fact that it is not so much key contrast which creates harmonic stress as the degree of vertical dissonance between parts. Whatever keys are used, consonances between parts will make for euphony, while dissonances will form different degrees of harshness according to frequency of use and degree of conflict.

Polytonality is music in more than two parts, when more than two keys are used together. Perhaps the most technically outstanding examples of this are Milhaud's string quartets Nos. 8 and 9, which can be played separately or together as an octet, with each instrument in a different key. I heard these played both as quartets and as an octet many years ago, and found the music surprisingly good and the idiom not unpleasant. Unfortunately, these unusual works are now rarely, if ever, played.

An excellent example of polytonality is the third movement of Hindemith's *Five Pieces for String Orchestra*, Op. 44. Virtually the whole movement comprises a double canon which begins as in the second violin and viola parts given in Example 90 (these parts first being played by first violin and viola):

Example 90: Hindemith: Five Pieces for String Orchestra

The point at which our example begins is the first entry of the full orchestra, with the first and second violins in one canon and the violas and basses in another. Each canon has the following voice (or 'consequent') only a quaver later and a semitone higher (if one disregards the fact that the basses are transposed down an octave). Apart from a central episode in two parts only, the whole movement follows the same pattern of double canons with the consequents a quaver later and a semitone higher.

The result is highly chromatic yet not excessively dissonant, because Hindemith took care of the vertical (chordal) combinations at every point. The harmony is in fact remarkably smooth throughout the piece, and is as rich and vital as one could wish. Polytonal music need not necessarily be brutal and discordant, provided the composer reconciles the horizontal flow of the various voices with the vertical results. (In Example 90, the triads are so frequently of the augmented type that it seems probable that the harmony was composed first and the horizintal outline of each voice delineated only afterwards. This seems an extraordinary procedure. Nevertheless, the craftsmanship revealed − whether the harmony is a casual result or a prime cause − is remarkable. One thing is certain: the full four-part double canon had to be composed before the composer could write the two parts of the first fifteen bars.)

A slightly different form of bitonal and polytonal usage is found where composers define a tonality strongly and then contradict it in some prominent way. This kind of tonal contradiction may not necessarily follow clear key patterns (as in bitonality and polytonality), but the idea of creating stress by note-conflict is very much the same. Example 91, from Britten's *War Requiem*, has a tenor recitative over a sustained chord of G minor (first inversion):

Example 91: Britten: *War Requiem*, VI Libera me

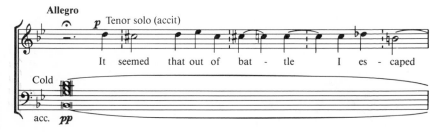

Ex. 91: (*cont.*)

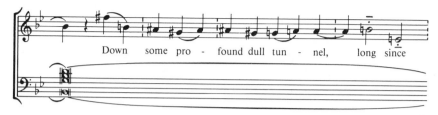

Down   some pro - found dull tun - nel,   long since

Scooped   through gra - nites   which ti - ta - nic   wars had   groined.

The tenor part is frequently in strong, discordant opposition to the accompaniment, but there does not seem to be any planned tonal scheme. However, occasional background chords are introduced (e.g. seventh chords on D, F♯, A♭, E, etc.) which though overlaying the G minor chord, momentarily agree — very loosely — with the voice part. The technique is really one of creating harmony in two separate and unrelated layers.

A much more unusual kind of tonal conflict is occasionally found where composers add one piece of music to another, as in the works of Charles Ives, where the strains of a military band or an organ may be added to the orchestra, in a different key and moving at a different tempo. In more recent times, Luciano Berio has used the same technique in his *Sinfonia*, *Labirintus II*, and electronic works, so that we seem to be hearing different music — symphonic, jazz, military, vocal, etc. — as if radios were tuned to different stations and the music merging, conflicting, and changing.

To sum up, bitonality and polytonality allow us to produce music which has a feeling of modernity, even though each voice may be simple and diatonic. The difficulty lies in creating good vertical results. The harmony should not normally be a random end product, beautiful at one moment and ugly the next. It should be carefully controlled so that it has the same character at all times, and is in perfect accord with the composer's aesthetic objectives.

Harmony in fourths

Harmony based on notes a perfect fourth apart ('quartal harmony') has been used by composers for almost the entire century, as a means of escaping from the old harmony based on thirds, with its complex systematization and expansion into the chromatic field. As harmony made by grouping notes in perfect fourths will inevitably eliminate thirds, the result sounds very different from conventional harmony; and as dominant–tonic chords cannot be formed, and there is no semitonal leading-note effect, the characteristic progressions of diatonicism are quite absent. In fact, like whole-tone harmony, the effect of quartal harmony is somewhat static and suited to tranquil moods. Probably Schoenberg was the first to exploit this system in his Chamber Symphony Op. 9 (1906). The piece begins with the horn solo given in Example 92:

Example 92: Schoenberg: Chamber Symphony Op. 9

Having first used fourths melodically, Schoenberg then combines them vertically, as harmony. At the beginning of the slow movement he writes a well intergrated combination of horizontal and vertical usages, with the fourth groupings centered on two different registers. In bar 3 the G♯ begins a 'transposed' group of fourths, while the second half of bar 4 returns to the first grouping, which then continues to the end of the example:

Example 93

Ex. 93: (*cont.*)

This 'transposition' of fourth groupings is almost the only way to avoid the continuous recurrence of the same notes, which could become obvious and stagnant. However, in the finale of his Six Small Piano Pieces Op. 19 Schoenberg contrived a different solution, which has the advantage of combining the smooth, static quality of harmony in fourths with the unexpected. Notes seem to be introduced which are outside the system, yet when we investigate his methods we find that what is seemingly haphazard is in reality well planned:

Example 94: Schoenberg: Six Small Piano Pieces, Op. 19

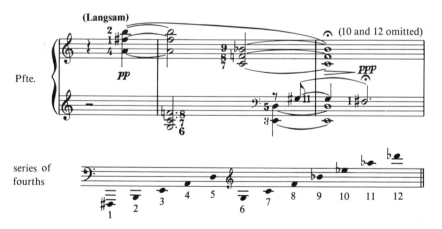

As will be seen, apart from grouping notes 6–9 normally, the rest is made up by omitting notes from chords and then introducing them later on. While notes 3 and 5 in the series of fourths are omitted at first, they later form a chord themselves, joined by note 11 (note 10 being omitted). The remaining notes (10 and 12) are introduced in the following bar.

In writing thus, Schoenberg must have been trying to hide the main defect in this kind of quartal harmony — its tendency to become over-obvious and mechanical. However, if we transpose notes into different octaves and use Schoenberg's method of omitting certain notes only to include them later on, we can disguise the system and the effect can be excellent.

So far, we have mostly considered the use of fourth chords in situations where only one vertical chord is built of perfect fourths superimposed, each note remaining in the same register. We have seen how difficult it is to gain a horizontal flow with such limited material, and that the resulting music is inevitably fairly static. To get the music moving horizontally and yet retain the essential character of quartal harmony, we have to take liberties and extend the system in some way. One method is to use 'inversions' of quartal chords, so that notes of the same chord are used in different registers. For instance, using only components of the quartal chord D, G, C, F, we can move as follows, by abandoning the strict use of fourths without transposition, and using the notes in different groupings and in different registers:

Example 95

In spite of the abandoning of strict usages of harmony in fourths, it will be felt that in the above example the same harmonic mood persists throughout. It is therefore possible to have real horizontal movement without disturbing the harmonic atmosphere.

One can also move to adjacent fourths, or even to fourth groups with completely new components. As an example, we begin below with the fourth group E, A, D, G, then include C and F, and then move on to F, Bb, Eb, and Ab, finally reversing the process to return to E, A, D and G:

Example 96

108

Another method of creating horizontal movement is to make partial use of scale structures, even though we may prefer to hide scale origins completely. Consider for a moment two ways of superimposing fourths on the scale of C major:

Example 97a

Example 97b

In order to create chords each having two perfect fourths as in (a), B♭ and E♭ have had to be introduced in the first and fourth chords. This is a clue to the inclusion of more chromaticism in the system. But, more important, in (b), where chromaticisms are not used, different kinds of fourth chords occur. On C we have a perfect fourth below and an augmented fourth above. On F these two intervals are inverted. These chords with augmented fourths are both strongly dissonant and can add considerably to the variety of harmonic colour available. The blandness of harmony in perfect fourths can, through including augmented fourths, be given a piquant force which many composers have found attractive. In fact, this augmented fourth chord is very frequently found as a predominant chord-shape in much of the music of composers such as Webern. Example 98 is made from elements in both (a) and (b) of the above — i.e. the notes B and B♭, E and E♭ are used:

Example 98

Finally, augmented fourth chords can, when combined, produce a powerful harmonic effect. Example 99, from my own Organ Symphony, combines two streams of fourth chords, mostly in counter-parallel motion. Most chords are

109

a combination of perfect fourth above and augmented fourth below, except for the introduction of sixths in the last chords of the left hand:

Example 99: Smith Brindle: *Organ Symphony*

In its 'pure' form, quartal harmony cannot easily be combined with other harmonic systems. It has its own special atmosphere, and, moreover, it is not easily spread over large areas without stagnation. It is therefore usually reserved for short pieces or episodes. However, if it is used in a freer, less pure form, it is very adaptable and merges well with chromatic idioms.

11 Technical expansions: 2

Towards atonality

As this is not a book dedicated only to twentieth-century harmony, it is important not to get too involved in lengthy harmonic discussions. It will be necessary to take many short cuts and leap over details which academics could wrangle over interminably. It is assumed that the student already knows enough about chromatic harmony, or has a sufficiently enquiring mind, to take the leap over the abyss of atonality in his stride.

'Atonality' means different things to different people. Originally, 'atonal' music was presumed to be music in which there was a complete absence of tonality. There was something pejorative about the word, so that to some atonal music meant 'non-music', or at least something ugly and unpleasant. To others it meant merely music not written in definite keys.

It would seem that the originators of atonality believed that their music was really completely non-tonal, but by now it can be seen that atonality is really an obscuring of tonalities in varying degrees. Sometimes the obscuring may be only slight, at other times considerable. The truth is that 'atonality' is in fact a mistaken term. Whenever two or more notes are put together, a harmonic and therefore 'tonal' relationship is created, be it simple or complex. In atonal music, the harmonic relationships may be very complex indeed, yet they are undoubtedly there. Much so-called 'atonal' music is only music with a tonal foundation so obscured or disrupted that it is not easily perceived. The only music which is really non-tonal is that based on chromatic clusters of semitones (or even smaller intervals), where no single tone can predominate. (If any note were to dominate it would create a tonal centre.)

There are two main ways of creating atonality: one is to begin with a tonal framework and then obscure it; the other is to ignore conventional harmonies altogether and use only note-combinations which do not suggest tonalities. We will leave the latter method until the section on free 12-note music below, as it is more difficult, beginning here with the method of obscuring tonalities. As well as being simpler, this allows us to follow a historical sequence which leads up to serialism. First we will deal with diatonic and chromatic substitution notes, which are the main means of obscuring conventional chords.

Substitution notes. The term 'substitution note' is not in normal use. It has had to be coined because no other term adequately describes its function. A substitution note is a note which takes the place of a harmony note immediately adjacent to it (sometimes above, sometimes below). It does not belong to the basic harmony, which it tends to disrupt. It may or may not resolve on to the note it temporarily replaces.

Substitution notes may be diatonic or chromatic. With a chord of C major, diatonic substitution notes would be as shown in Example 100, resolving on the note substituted as indicated (if any resolution takes place):

Example 100

The above resolutions may not take place at all; indeed, one substitution note may move to another (presuming the same harmony), again without any resolution taking place.

Chromatic substitution notes in C major would be as shown in Example 101, again showing possible resolutions on the notes substituted:

Example 101

These chromatic notes may alternatively be written as C#, E♭, G♭, G#, and B♭ (or A#), at the composer's discretion.

A very simple and beautiful example of the use of substitution notes may be found at the beginning of Wagner's *Tristan und Isolde*:

Example 102: Wagner: *Tristan und Isolde*, Prelude, Act I

Here the commonplace cadence A minor–F7–E7 is given a subtle mystery through the use of a few substitution notes as follows: in bar 2, G♯ is a chromatic substitution for A (on which it resolves), while B is a diatonic substitution for A or C, on which it does not resolve; in bar 3, A♯ substitutes chromatically for B, on which it resolves.

Example 103, from No. 7 of Karg-Elert's *Interludes in Various Keys* for organ, shows a mixture of diatonic and chromatic substitution notes typical of this composer:

Example 103: Karg-Elert: *Organ Interludes: No. 7*

The student will be able to analyse this for himself, but he should beware of treating the second chord in the penultimate bar, or the first chord in the last bar, as triads in their own right. These are no more than substitution notes decorating the main harmonies. (Note how one of these is identical to the first *Tristan* chord (Example 102), with the addition of the bass D.) One peculiarity to be observed is the leap B–G♯ from one substitution note to another in the melody.

Example 104 is taken from Percy Scholes's *Oxford Companion to Music* (8th edn), where it is quoted as music which 'abandons all pretence of key in any strand whatever', and is therefore completely atonal:

Example 104: Schoenberg: Three Piano Pieces, Op. 11

However, far from being atonal, the upper part is very clearly in G minor — G♯ being merely a substitution note for A, on which it resolves (an octave lower than usual). The first chord in the left hand can be read as F♯, E, and G♯, so that G♯ is a substitution note for A. This bar then contains a 9th chord on D (which is itself omitted) — the dominant chord for the final bar. Of course, the final bar is a 7th chord on G with both major and minor thirds present. Far from there being 'no pretence of key', this is a very straightforward dominant–tonic cadence, a little obscured but really very simple.

Atonality

As the number of substitution notes is increased and their resolutions are omitted, so do tonalities become more and more obscured and disrupted. This does not mean that the music becomes ugly or excessively dissonant. In Example 105 Schoenberg creates a beautifully delicate harmony, which seems to float along on a distant astral plane. At times tonal zones can be identified; at others they are elusive, but in their sum tonalities are so well hidden that we can regard this as truly 'atonal' (in the sense of being tonally obscure):

Example 105: Schoenberg: Six Little Piano Pieces, Op. 19

It would be laborious to analyse this note by note, but there are several principal features which can be noted:

(1) There is a great deal of scalic movement, though it is mostly hidden by notes leaping out of direction and back again. For example, one can trace an octave descent of semitones from the top Gb in bar 2.

(2) Here and there triadic chords (in 7th or 9th form) are fairly clear. For example, the quotation begins on C minor, while on the fifth beat in bar 2 there is a straightforward chord of D9. Bar 3 begins with root position chords of F and A in major and minor form (obscured of course, by substitution notes).

(3) Groups of semitones are used at various points, or notes from semitone groups may be spread by inversions, creating the most tonally obscure situations. For example, on the last beat in bar 2 the notes comprise five adjacent semitones from C♯ to F (even though they are spread out). In the last bar, there are three semitone groups — E, D♯, D♮, F, F♯, G (top stave), and C♯, D, Eb (bottom stave). The latter two groups are used in such a way that, vertically, there are semitonal conflicts at almost every moment.

(4) There is prominent use of parallelisms and counter-parallelisms. For example, in the first left-hand chord, the top part moves up and down a semitone, while the bottom two parts do the opposite. The last bar is full of counter-movement, both in semitones and thirds. It would seem certain that this last bar has been constructed on a basis of counter-parallelisms rather than on any tonal scheme.

(5) The use of octaves is rare — a common feature of all atonal music.

(6) The composer makes fairly consistent use of all twelve chromatic notes. To take samples, the first two beats of the example comprise nine different notes out of ten; the second phrase beginning in bar 2 (fifth beat) has seven different notes out of ten; while the final bar has ten different notes out of thirteen (different octave registers are, of course, disregarded). These samples reveal the composer's purpose — to use the total-chromatic fairly consistently and, by so doing, create constant disruptions of tonal centres.

Free chromaticism or free twelve-note music

We have already pointed out that atonal music can be written not by obscuring tonal structures but by ignoring conventional harmonies altogether and using only note-combinations which avoid the suggestion of tonalities. Already, in Example 105, several zones (especially those based on semitone clusters) were obviously composed through this method of working with non-tonal note combinations.

Normally, this method of 'free chromaticism', or 'free twelve-note composition', is used for highly chromatic music which avoids tonal suggestions and uses all twelve notes of the total-chromatic fairly consistently. This is a rather complex technique of composition. The concept of freedom is here completely illusory, and the compositional system is bound by as many rules and prohibitions as is conventional music. It would need an entire book to discuss the system adequately. Nevertheless, we will attempt here to outline the main principles as simply as possible, without discussing complex issues. In any case, this mode of composition is still in a fluid state, and no textbook seems to exist which one can regard as completely authoritative. So what follows is an extreme simplification of many complex matters, given as an introduction to a system which the student has largely to discover for himself.

As the purpose of writing free twelve-note music is to eliminate the main characteristics of conventional tonal music, there are several simple principles to observe:

(1) The use of conventional scales must be avoided. Similarly, horizontal note movements (melodic or otherwise) must not resemble scale patterns. Inevitably, melodies often contain more leaps than in conventional music, or there may be a good deal of semitonal movement or inversions of semitones to create such intervals as 7ths and minor 9ths.

(2) Triadic groups such as major and minor chords should not be used, nor 7th, 9th, or diminished 7th chords. (Occasionally these latter are used if they are incomplete and passed over quickly so as to be inconspicuous.)

(3) Any chord sequence resembling a conventional cadence must be avoided.

(4) The total-chromatic of twelve different notes within the octave must be used continuously, though their order may constantly change. However, it is common for fewer than twelve notes to be used over specific areas, or for certain notes to be repeated or used more than others, as long as the general non-tonal effect is maintained.

(5) Non-conventional music must avoid conventional rhythmic designs, or the music will retain a traditional character.

A quotation from Bartók's Fourth String Quartet will serve to confirm the above principles (Example 106, next page). Neither scales nor conventional chords or cadences are used. The first two-bar phrase uses all twelve semitones except Ab.

On these factors, one could make several observations. Brief scale segments are suggested in bar 2 (first and second violins), but the harsh dissonances between these two parts creates such a degree of non-tonality that the scale effect is obscured. Bar 1 is less dissonant than the rest, and

Example 106: Bartók: Quartet No. 4, 1st movt.

contains very brief quasi-triadic groups such as the diminished 7th chord C, E♭, F♯, and the following minor 9th and minor 7th chords on the last beat. Note how in the remainder of the quotation, semitone clashes are very frequent, with three adjacent semitones on beats 1 and 2 of bar 2. The last chord is the most triadic — a minor chord with a major 7th. The second phrase comprises only eight different notes, but this is because the parts are close together in a small area, and some notes are used by two different instruments.

The principle of 'leaping melody' is not apparent in the above example, as Bartók's melodic construction is here based on movement within a small area. Example 107 gives a melody from a solo piece in the free twelve-note manner, rather florid and virtuoso in style:

Example 107: Donatoni: *Algo* for guitar

Note the rhythmic irregularity and lack of classical rhythmic shapes. Large leaps make for a very jagged contour, and the total-chromatic is fairly evenly spread, though there is an occasional recurrence of small note-groups.

Twelve-note harmony

The most complex aspect of free chromaticism is that of harmony. One could dismiss this factor once and for all merely by saying that any aspect of conventional harmony (triadic chords, cadences, etc.) must be avoided. But this leaves the student with the highly enigmatic problem of how to deal with the mass of unconventional note-combinations within the total-chromatic. Some may sound well at all times; some may sound good or bad according to various circumstances; while others may sound ugly wherever they are placed. Then there is the problem of a satisfactory flow from one note-combination to another. In short, we still have to deal with a harmonic problem — the satisfactory effect of note-combinations both in isolation and in horizontal movement. As this 12-note harmony cannot be discussed through the rules of conventional harmony, we have to discover our own methods.

Conflicting notes. We will discuss here two different methods which have the advantage that they can be combined into a more comprehensive system. The simplest method is that of using conflicting or contradicting notes, so that tonal groups are disrupted or the influence of even a single tone nullified. The example from Bartók's Fourth Quartet illustrates this method, which must have been the composer's way of working in many parts of the work. The first bar, beginning with E and C, would seem set to create a tonality of C major, but this is immediately contradicted by the F–F♯ of the first violin. The E♭ of the second violin further contradicts the impression of C major, moving to F with A in the cello. This seems to suggest F major, but this is in turn contradicted by the F♯ and D♯ of the first violin. Next, the three parts form a cluster (F♯, F♮, E) which moves through the conflicting D and E♭ to another cluster (D, D♭, C). The phrase ends on a final ambiguous chord — B♭, E♭, B♮. In the following bars the conflict is even greater, as the note relationships are closer — tones and semitones. Of course, we must not presume that the use of conflicting notes was Bartók's only consideration. For example, he was working out the exposition of the melodic cells which are the basis of most of the movement, so that his use of contradicting notes had to fit in with the melodic intervals, which were probably his primary concern.

We will now briefly investigate means of forming harmony of a moderately non-tonal nature in up to five parts by using contradicting notes. First of all, we will use the total-chromatic in a succession of consonant two-note groups (Example 108):

Example 108

Our next step is to form three-part harmony by adding a note to each chord which is dissonant with one of the existing notes. This means that the added contradicting note must be a major or minor 2nd (or 7th or 9th) distant from either existing note:

Example 109

To form four-part harmony we now add a lower part which again contradicts an upper part except in the fifth chord. Here there is no contradiction, because the bass is consonant with all the upper notes. However, this chord fits in well with the others because the strength of discord is equal to that in other chords:

Example 110

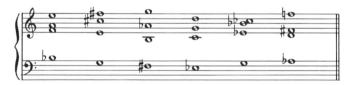

Finally we add a low part to make five-part harmony. Note how in the first chord the bass is consonant with all the upper parts, while in the others it is dissonant with one or more upper parts. In the last chord the bass is in conflict with all three upper parts, yet this is probably the most tonal-sounding chord, with its resemblance to a chord of E9:

Example 111

Each of these chords sounds reasonably well, and the harmonic flow from chord to chord is good. This is because of the even use of the whole total-chromatic, the fairly open spacing, and the tendency to place strong consonances in lower parts. There is no doubt that with closer spacing and dissonances in the lower parts the same note-groups could produce ugly results. We will return to this problem of spacing in the following section, with a more extended discussion on consonance and dissonance.

The second method of creating harmony in free twelve-note music is mostly concerned with the qualities of intervals (their different degrees of consonance or dissonance), their combination in chords, and the control of the horizontal flow of such chords. We will therefore call this method of harmony creation 'interval harmony'.

Interval harmony. Example 112 shows consonant intervals within the octave, with the strongest on the left moving to the weakest on the right:

Example 112

Apart from the unison, it will be seen that consonances consist really of only three intervals (5ths and major and minor 3rds) and their inversions. The inversion of the unison (the octave) is omitted, because it is largely avoided in twelve-note music through its tendency to dominate as a tonal centre.

Though we have begun by stating that some consonances are stronger than others, the difference is not striking, and for the sake of simplicity we intend to regard them as equal for this method of creating harmony. However, the remaining intervals have very different qualities:

Example 113

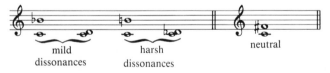

mild dissonances · harsh dissonances · neutral

Dissonances based on the major 2nd and its inversions (minor 7th and major 9th) are milder than the harsh effect of the semitone and its inversions (major 7th and minor 9th). Again, we are only really concerned with two intervals and their inversions, but it must be noticed that one is much more dissonant than the other. With inversions, the degree of dissonance is much attenuated.

The tritone, though designated as 'neutral', has a rather changeable quality, as it can seem mildly dissonant in a consonant context or consonant in a dissonant one. However, for the sake of simplicity, we can regard the tritone as being midway between consonant and dissonant.

Our first step in illustrating interval harmony using the whole chromatic octave will be to write a succession of consonances in two parts:

Example 114

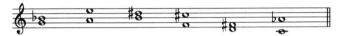

This succession of six two-part chords uses the total-chromatic and a variety of consonances, though not the 4th and major 6th. We will now add a lower part which will turn the consonant effect into one of uniformly relaxed mild dissonance. This is done in each chord by adding a note which is mildly dissonant with one of the upper parts. The mild dissonance used is either a minor 7th or a major 9th:

Example 115

Note that the added part is mostly in contrary motion with the top part (this usually gives a more powerful bass), and that all the notes used are different. These two factors will also be characteristic of other examples which follow.

Our next step will be to show how the same two-part chords of Example 114 can be given much more tension through harsh dissonances added in a lower part:

Example 116

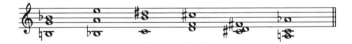

The lower part is always a semitone or a major 7th from an upper part. Again, there is no note repetition and the movement is mostly in contrary motion with the treble.

In the following examples we will alter the above procedure, beginning with two-part chords which are all dissonant. We have included tritones as mild dissonances deliberately, to illustrate certain factors:

Example 117

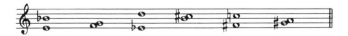

We will now introduce a lower part which will disperse the dissonances in the upper parts and produce relatively smooth, relaxed harmony. This is done most efficiently when the lower part is consonant with both the upper parts:

Example 118

Note that with tritones, the only possible notes which are consonant with both upper parts cause incomplete diminished 7th chords to appear.

Finally, we will add a fourth part below to make complete four-part harmony. We will set ourselves the objective of increasing the degree of consonance still further, and therefore the bass will be kept consonant with all upper parts:

Example 119

Though the effect of this is quite good, indeed smooth and sonorous, the concept of using a bass consonant with all upper parts has produced chords which are either diminished 7ths (chord 1) or contain major or minor chords. (Note that in chord 1 a tritone has been used as a consonance. This could also have been done in the penultimate chord, but we have chosen to avoid it by using a bass (E) which is mildly dissonant with an upper note (F#).)

It could well be that for some musical purposes the above result may contain too great an element of consonance in the form of triads. In this case a bass line must be chosen which avoids the forming of an excess of conventional triads and yet gives just the right harmonic equilibrium:

Example 120

(In the above example, so as to follow the 'step-by-step' method of our exposition, we have deliberately avoided any alteration to the tenor part, and confined our changes to the bass only. However, in practice, better results would be obtained by reviewing both lower parts freely, without following the stricter method we have used.)

A word about the spacing of parts. Dissonances are most acute when the dissonant voices are close together. If we wish to attenuate dissonances we should therefore separate them adequately. If we wish them to be strong we should bring the notes close together. The consonance of intervals is also dissipated by distance. Another factor is that the characteristics of intervals are greatly increased in the low registers and decreased in the upper. It is particularly important to avoid placing dissonant intervals, especially 2nds, in low registers, unless we deliberately wish to create a brutal, harsh effect. Consider again the natural harmonic series (mentioned in Chapter 10, 'Free Diatonicism'): the most consonant intervals are in the low registers, well apart, and as intervals become more dissonant they move into higher registers, where dissonance is hardly noticed. If we wish to have a euphonious, smooth-sounding harmony, we should do the same — consonances spread out below, dissonances above. However, we can by no means stick slavishly to such a rule, for good harmonic flow needs variety in spacing intervals, and in any case we may wish to avoid smooth harmony and have something pungent, harsh, and bitter. The right spacing of voices and placing of intervals is therefore of paramount importance in acheiving our aesthetic objectives.

By now it should be obvious that with interval harmony it is possible to obtain whatever harmonic results we please, through the manipulation of the consonant or dissonant intervals available to us, without resorting to tonal conventions. We have seen how a couple of strands of consonant voices can be turned into mild or harsh dissonance, or vice versa — how dissonant voices can be turned towards consonance. We can therefore create whatever degree of atonal norm we wish, just through our knowledge of the nature of intervals.

There is, however, one important factor to be clarified. Our examples have been confined to simple homophonic chords in which all the notes sound together. But in real music this happens only rarely. Much more frequently, notes overlap, one part being sustained while another moves over two or more notes, as in the upper stave of Example 121. Here the upper parts move together at only one point; at all others they overlap. The bass part has therefore been added according to the principles of interval harmony, so as to maintain the right equilibrium of consonance and dissonance. As it happens, the bass part has been designed so that the result is relatively consonant and relaxed, but it would have been equally easy (as we have shown above) to make it contribute more dissonance and tension:

Example 121

etc.

One important principle must be observed: important parts should be composed first, and the supporting part or parts added later to create satisfactory harmony. In this way a good horizontal flow is far more certain than if one were constantly preoccupied with assessing the vertical results of each note combination, as was the case in the 'contradicting note' method. Interval harmony is therefore to be recommended not only because it encourages the horizontal flow of parts and their final resolution into good harmony, but also because the process gives quicker and easier results. In any case, it is much better to compose 'moving forward' rather than thinking vertically, which inhibits good horizontal lines. Nevertheless, the 'contradicting note' method of working is so close to the system of 'interval harmony' that in some circumstances the two systems can be used together. In fact, once we have gained adequate facility, we need concern ourselves no longer with method, and all our faculties can be concentrated on the task of creation. With experience we control harmonic factors almost by instinct, knowing at a glance what is good and what is not without having to resort to rules and reasonings.

12 Serialism

It is hardly possible to give a thumbnail sketch of serialism for it is a complex compositional system which would require an entire volume for its full exposition. However, it would help the student if he were introduced to it briefly and with simplicity, not only because a knowledge of serialism is essential to an understanding of today's music, but also because so many aspects of it can enrich other methods of composition, even in other styles and idioms.

In addition, serialism can be very helpful in a special way. The series offer us basic material on which the creative mind can work right from the beginning of a composition, with the result that the imagination often responds by producing fruitful ideas quickly. In other words, the note patterns of a series serve as a stimulus to the imagination, and creative ideas leap to the mind in abundance once we begin to work. One of the chief characteristics of much serial music is frequent change, and it is therefore fortunate that the method itself favours abundant ideas.

The series

Serialism has as its prime objective an organized way of composing with all the twelve notes contained within the octave. The order of these is established in a 'series'[1] which recurs constantly throughout a work, so that all the notes of the total-chromatic are used evenly to maintain an atonal atmosphere. Some composers use series which may contain more or fewer notes than the twelve contained in the total-chromatic, but this is uncommon, and the usage can be ignored. We will therefore examine first a typical series of twelve notes:

Example 122: Berg: Andante from the Lyric Suite

[1] 'Tone-row' (US) and 'note-row' are also often used.

The series is not a theme but a sequence of notes, so it is usually written out as above in equal note values. Also, it must be understood that the notes written represent all analogous notes in any octave (for instance, the first note E stands for any E within the range of audibility).

Melodic series

Some series are designed from the moment of conception to have primarily melodic potential, their contours suggesting a good melodic flow. The series by Berg shown in Example 122 was obviously designed to give a lyrical melodic sweep to the melody in the second movement of his Lyric Suite for string quartet:

Example 123

It will be noted that Berg's series contains three distinct tonal groups: minor chords on D♯ and F, and four notes from G to D within the tonal zone of G. However, tonal factors are less essential to a good melodic series than variety of intervals and memorable interval relationships.

Atonal series

Because series are meant to produce atonality they usually lack tonal suggestions, as in Example 124:

Example 124: Webern: Symphony, Op. 21

In this series no group of three adjacent notes has any tonal suggestion. The note-groups are of four kinds: two adjacent semitones; or semitones added to a tone, a minor 3rd, or a 4th. It is obvious that, heard horizontally, this series on its own would give no tonal impression, and if any group of three or more notes is used vertically as a chord the effect is bound to be dissonant and non-tonal. However, there is one major defect: used horizontally, repetitions of the series would create a 9th chord on G with notes 11, 12, 1, 2, and 3, an eventuality which must naturally be avoided.

Symmetrical series

Note that the second half of the above series is the same as the first in reverse, but transposed. This is therefore a 'symmetrical' series, of which there are various kinds — notably, mirror series (as above), series made up of transpositions of three or four note-groups comprising the same interval successions, series made of retrogrades and inversions of a small note-cell, and symmetrical all-interval series which comprise all intervals within the octave.

Tonal series

Tonal suggestions in series have already been mentioned above in connection with Berg's series from the Lyric Suite. Tonal series are designed to contain note-groups of a triadic nature, or to have a whole group of notes in the same key. However, the objective is not to produce one constant tonality, but rather to create chromatic harmony in which brief hints of triadic harmony mingle with note-combinations of a more obscure nature. The result, which can be a subtle amalgam of tonality and atonality, is singularly beautiful in the hands of composers such as Berg and Dallapiccola. We will illustrate this with Dallapiccola's *Quaderno musicale di Annalibera*, previously discussed in connection with whole-tone usages (Example 86). The series is as shown in Example 125:

Example 125: Dallapiccola: *Quaderno musicale di Annalibera*

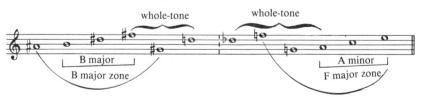

Two triads (B major and A minor) are very evident, while two groups of three and four notes each comprise notes from the two possible whole-tone scales (which, as we have seen, can form harmony of a pleasant, elusive quality).

Perhaps more important still, each half of the series has a large five-note group in the zones of B and F. Note that these zones, being a tritone apart, are tonally as far apart as is possible. This in itself guarantees a constant contradiction of tonal effects, whenever these emerge. Note that the Dallapiccola series is much richer in intervals than the series of Webern's Symphony — in fact all intervals within the octave except 4ths and 5ths can be obtained from this series. This wide variety of intervals is an important factor in making this series very fruitful in melodic potential.

Derived forms of the series

The series in its first form is usually called the 'original', or 'O', form, or sometimes the 'basic set'. When this form is used backwards it is called the 'retrograde', or 'R', form. In the 'inversion', or 'I', form, all intervals of the 'O' version are inverted, while the 'retrograde of the inversion' ('RI') is the 'I' version backwards. Using the series from Webern's Symphony, the four forms are as shown in Example 126:

Example 126

Transposed forms of the series

As each series can be transposed to begin on any note of the chromatic scale, there are twelve different 'O' versions and, in addition, twelve each of the 'I',

'R', and 'RI' versions — a total of forty-eight. (However, in a symmetrical series such as that quoted above, certain transpositions of 'R' can be the same as forms of 'O'. Similarly some transpositions of 'I' will be duplicated in those of 'RI'. There are therefore only twenty-four possible note-orders in such a symmetrical series.)

Though each series has normally forty-eight forms, it is rare for a composer to use them all. In fact composers often use only the original series, its derived forms, and perhaps two or three transpositions. These are enough for quite extended works.

Writing melody

Serial music may be written in various idioms, some of which may have virtually no melody at all. Other idioms may be based on melody of widely different kinds, spanning from almost traditional thematic characteristics to melody which has hardly any element of tradition. We will try to illustrate these possibilities with just a few examples, though it is naturally impossible to cover the subject adequately in a short space.

Melodic characteristics depend on a composer's idiom, and in turn are chief elements in the formation of that idiom. One of the main factors, in creating melody and in determining an idiom is that of rhythmic shape. Rhythms are completely dominant in determining the characteristics of a melody. Note-successions can be exactly the same (as in the series), but it is their rhythmic configuration which determines whether they form melody of classical or completely non-classical character.

Serial melody of a traditional character clearly needs rhythmic outlines of conventional shape. The following Aria from Dallapiccola's opera *Il prigioniero* has equal eight-beat phrase-lengths throughout (indicated by dotted slurs) and is made up of three rhythmic elements: repeated crotchets, occasional pairs of quavers, and the dotted rhythm, which occurs only twice:

Example 127: Dallapiccola: *Il prigioniero*

Ex. 127: *(cont.)*

scel - li,   lie - ti in   vol - to,   i   Pez - zen - ti   pas - so - no.

This thematic material (which recurs frequently in the opera) comprises a series which begins on C and covers the first five full bars. The remainder is a retrograde of the same series a semitone lower. Note that, as far as the rhythmic design is concerned, this could be Beethoven, whose Ode to Joy in the Ninth Symphony has exactly the same rhythmic elements, disposed differently. However, the chromaticism of the series breaks up the association with classicism to a large degree. This example illustrates that notes can be repeated in a melody, and that one can re-use a previous note which has already been passed over. In fact it is possible to repeat entire serial note-groups and thereby give the theme more definition (Example 128):

Example 128: Smith Brindle: *Via Crucis*

Note the repetition of note-groups and individual notes, which allow one to 'stretch out' the music so that the series covers a fair area, resulting in music of greater definition and memorability than would otherwise be possible.

Moving away from traditional melody, the main characteristic of serialism is the non-repetition of rhythms. Example 129 is typical of serial melody, in which perpetual change is the dominant rule. No rhythm is repeated, and every event is novel:

Example 129: Maderna: Oboe Concerto

Inevitably, this gives thematic material of a very fleeting nature. Even though it is intense, lyrical, and momentarily expressive, there is so much change that nothing precise can be recalled.

This thematic indefinition was a characteristic of Webern, who was such an inspiration to young composers in the post-war period. Example 130 is the theme of the Variations in his Symphony Op. 21:

Example 130: Webern: Symphony, Op. 21

This is an extremely logical construction. We already know that the series (Example 126) is of a symmetrical 'mirror' type, the last six notes being a transposed retrograde of the first six. The theme uses each half of the series so that there is not only a transposed pitch retrograde at the midway point (halfway through bar 6) but also a rhythmic retrograde. In other words, the theme of eleven bars has rhythms that turn backwards at the mid point. Note that even the dynamics are mirrored. Now this theme happens to be one of Webern's most memorable instrumental conceptions, yet it is very elusive, probably because of its poorly defined rhythmic shape. Perhaps Webern was aiming at just such a lack of definition, and certainly many composers have been attracted by this very quality, as well as by his intellectualism, over the last thirty years.

Example 131 is very typical of non-traditional melody in a rather disjointed style. Note the strong dynamic contrasts, large leaps, and tendency towards destruction of the metrical pulse; the music has continuity, but it is not effected by a sense of 'beat':

Example 131: Berio: *Serenata 1*

We have shown some rather extreme examples of traditional and non-traditional melody. Between these extremes are many possibilities. It is up to each of us to discover our own preferred means of expression, and this is best done by seeing the work of others. Example 132 shows just a few melodies of contrasting types:

Example 132: Gerhard: String Quartet

Stravinsky: *Threni*

Guitar

Schoenberg: Quartet No. 3

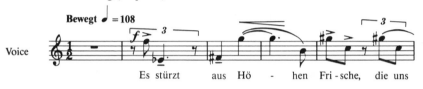

Vn. 1

Webern: Three Songs, Op. 23, No. 2

Voice

Es stürzt   aus Hö - hen Fri - sche, die uns

le - ben macht: das   Herz - blut   ist die Feuch - te

Pousseur: *Quintette*

Cl.

Melody and accompaniment

It is clearly impossible to discuss this subject exhaustively here, so we will be content with illustrating only three contrasting methods. Example 133 shows a simple chordal harmonization:

Example 133: Dallapiccola: *Quaderno*

The melody is an 'I' version of Example 125, beginning on B♭, and the accompaniment 'RI', beginning on E♭. Note the alterations in note-order of 'RI' in order to place each whole-tone group in turn in bars 3 and 4. C♯ is note 9 of both forms of the series. The harmony is very smooth, very close to chromatic tonal harmony. In Example 134 the accompaniment gives minimal harmonic support for the voice, taking as its objective instead the creation of movement:

Example 134: Webern: *Three Songs*, Op. 23, No. 2

Ex. 134: (*cont.*)

Movement is created by Webern's common practice of using counterpoints made of small rhythmic cells which are mirrored. Note how the right hand plays the rhythm ♩ ♪ ♫♫ and then its exact mirror in the next bar. Meanwhile the left hand plays the same rhythms in the opposite order. As the series is shared between the two parts, the note successions are varied and are not mirrored. Most of this song proceeds in the same manner.

Example 135 shows a very simple but effective way of creating movement and harmony at the same time. The repeating shape of the accompaniment in quavers is designed to recur only at the first beat of the seventh bar. The series is also spread over a broad area (both instruments sharing the same serial form) to cover the first twelve bars of the work. This gives the piece its calm harmonic stability:

Example 135: Bartolozzi: *Serenata*

Polyphony

All conventional polyphonic forms are well suited to serial composition, especially as the series is naturally suited to horizontal writing. Though fugue is regarded as too tonal a form to be of any use, many other old contrapuntal devices of the Renaissance and Baroque periods have been revived in serial composition, especially canon in its many forms. Example 136 is a simple two-part canon, the 'consequent' or following voice being a minor 6th below the leading voice:

Example 136: Stravinsky: *Threni*

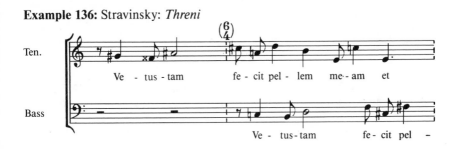

Example 137 is much more complex. Referring to the theme of Webern's Variations from the Symphony Op. 21 (Example 130), it will be recalled that this forms a mirrored structure both rhythmically and in note pitches (transposed). The first variation begins as follows, as a double canon by inversion:

Example 137: Webern: Symphony, Op. 21

The first canon by inversion is between the outer parts. At the halfway point (shown by a vertical dotted line) the parts move backwards in retrograde to end exactly as they began, thus making a 'mirror' form (as in all the succeeding variations and coda). The serial usage is arranged so that in the first half, the 'O', 'I', 'R', and 'RI' versions are all used at once, as follows: Violin 1 − 'O' beginning on C; Violin 2 − 'R' of the same series as that of Violin 1; Viola − 'RI' of the series beginning on B♭; Cello − 'I' of the series beginning on B♭. Naturally, as the second half of the variations is a retrograde of the first half, all the above are then reversed.

We would like to draw attention to the very simple rhythmic structure of this double canon. Both canons are made of similar material: cells of one, two, or three quavers, and the use of one or two crotchets. This material is not distinguished and memorable — perhaps deliberately, for the fugitive, enigmatic effect permeates the entire symphony. This subtle, indeterminate quality was Webern's ideal. (We will return to this subject later.)

Having introduced the reader to a fairly complex canonic structure we must move on, listing only a few main canonic usages as a reminder: canons at the unison, octave, and transposed; canon by inversion and canon by retrograde and inverted retrograde; canon cancrizans (mirrored canon as in Example 137); canons by diminution and augmentation. The last-named are useful in creating faster movement or in extending the material into slow sections, thus giving those speed changes which make more extended forms possible.

Rhythmic counterpoints and canons are similar to the above, but with the parts imitated in their rhythmic aspect only, ignoring the note-successions and intervals of the leading voice. We have already seen a form of this in the accompaniment to Webern's song in Op. 23 quoted above (Example 134).

Free counterpoints are common enough in serialism, the various voices in polyphony being made up of different rhythmic designs. Composers use them frequently, in order to avoid the rigidity of true canonic writing. With free counterpoint it is possible also to vary the number of 'parts' to form chords of different densities at any point, so that each horizontal line can be made up of vertical combinations of various numbers of notes. This can produce music of some density and apparent complexity through relatively simple means, as Example 138, based on the series of Webern's Op. 21, illustrates:

Example 138

Proportionalisms

Polyphonic music using brief rhythmic cells based on numerical proportions has already been illustrated in Example 61, where the accompaniment is based on the durational proportions 2:1:1 and the retrograde 1:1:2. Such proportions can be set to brief (producing rapid note-successions) or long (giving slow-moving counterpoints) durations. The musical result is usually somewhat enigmatic and intangible, and inevitably one piece of music tends to resemble another.

General comment on polyphony

Though clear canonic forms may be intelligible and easy to follow, the less obvious the forms used the more enigmatic and elusive the result. It is easy enough to be obscure and esoteric, much more difficult to be lucid and memorable to all. These considerations should be borne in mind, as they can determine the ultimate destiny of our music.

Serial usages

In order to illustrate various ways of using the series, we will use the 'O', 'I', 'R', and 'RI' forms of Webern's Op. 21 series as shown in Example 126. In the main, there are two principal methods of serial usage: one is to use the series in horizontal streams; the other in the 'horizontal-vertical' method.

Using horizontal streams, the simplest procedure is to write successions of the same series in each voice. Example 139 shows three-part counterpoint at the octave using the same 'O' series in each part:

Example 139

However, as repetitions of the same series can produce a lack of note-variety, it is usual to employ varied forms of a series (derived forms or transpositions). This produces that variety of note-successions so typical of the total-chromatic usage of serialism (Example 140):

Example 140

This exercise has been written in such a way as to reveal the considerable difficulty which inevitably occurs when using several serial forms at the same time. Whereas the serial usage of Example 139 (the same series in each voice) easily avoids the occurrence of octaves, octaves are formed only too easily when we use different forms together, as on the second quaver of the last bar, where all voices sound D♯ or E♭.

Octaves should be avoided in serial music for two reasons: first, they cause a note to sound out strongly as a tonal centre, disturbing the atonal equilibrium; secondly, in a succession of 'atonal' intervals the octave sounds weak and can cause a defective void in the harmonic flow. Serial composers generally avoid octaves altogether, and it is to be noted that meticulous workers such as Webern always contrive to form unisons when the same note occurs in two parts. However, the formation of unisons is not always satisfactory or possible (for example, in Example 140 above each voice could hardly be made to play the same unison D♯, for contrapuntal reasons, nor could it sound completely satisfactory).

The student may well ask what is the solution to this problem. If we wish to be true to the principles of serialism, we must be so meticulous in our work and choice of serial forms that the octave problem does not occur. If we are of a lazier disposition, the solution is simple and usually quite acceptable: if the same note will occur in two or more parts it can be omitted where it is least necessary and retained only in the principal part (thus in Example 140 we would keep the E♭ only in the upper voice, to retain the melodic shape).

In the horizontal-vertical method of serial usage we will first consider simple harmonic situations. Assuming four-part harmony, the series of Example 126 can be used vertically in descending order, as in (a), or ascending order, as in (b). In (c) each part is formed from a segment of the series, the soprano using notes 1–3, the alto 4–6, etc. (Example 141):

Example 141

(a) ⊙ of Webern Symphony
descending order

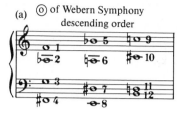

(b) ascending order

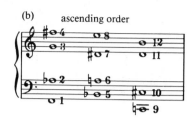

(c) horizontal segments

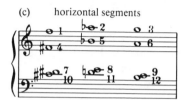

In Example 142 the horizontal-vertical method is used differently, each note in turn, in whatever voice or register, following the serial order. Note that where voices occur simultaneously strict ordering downwards has been used. However, composers very frequently use a free ordering of the note-material at such points:

Example 142

This is an excellent method of serial usage, and because it can produce a varied horizontal flow of notes in each part, a single version of a series can be used for a long piece (Luigi Nono's choral-orchestral work *Il canto sospeso*, for example, is written entirely with one series, never transposed and always in its 'O' form).

Alternatively, it is very fruitful to form long chains of (say) forty-eight notes, using four different versions of the series. In this way there is always an abundant amount of note-material available and one is able to obtain musical continuity easily. (Many serial writers — not only students — seem to write in twelve-note groups, the music being compartmented within the confines of each recurrence of series. This can hardly make for distinguished results.)

Serial harmony

In the above illustrations of serial usages it will be obvious that the harmony does not sound well — in fact Example 141(c) is quite vile. Perhaps harmonies such as these could form a suitable accompaniment to a horror film, but normally one would avoid such cacophony.

This brings us to the problem of whether to leave serial harmony as it is, the product of a system, or to override the system and make the harmonic result our own. There is no doubt whatever that many serial composers disregard the harmonic factor completely. For them the problem does not exist. For others the harmony must be a perfect expression of their aesthetic aims, and must therefore be of a uniformly specific quality — delicate or strong, mellifluous or pungent, arid or sweet. Every composer has his own ideals, and what sounds well to one may be anathema to another.

It is therefore certain that serial harmony, to suit a broad spectrum of different aesthetics, must be adapted to our individual needs. The question is whether it is really adaptable. It is certainly not if we keep to rigid serial usages, but with only a little modification we may produce harmonic results which suit well enough. For example, the brutal effect of Example 141(c) can be changed considerably if we dispose the vertical components of each chord differently:

Example 143

Here, the harshness of the original, with its dissonant 2nds and 7ths, has been converted to much less discordant chord-successions. Of course we have had to give up the strict ordering of the series in horizontal segments, but the actual notes in each chord are the same.

Many authorities would say that such a reordering of the series does not accord with serial principles; yet on the other hand one can point out that serialism is only a method established for the facilitation of composition using the total-chromatic. The method itself is no guarantee of artistic quality. If it produces poor results, it is surely legitimate to make changes. What matters is the quality of our music. If serialism has to be modified to suit our own expression, so be it.

The principles of making good serial harmony have already been largely covered in Chapter 11 ('Free chromaticism and free twelve-note music'). At first we outlined as our objective the elimination of the main characteristics of conventional tonal music by the following means: (1) we should avoid the use of conventional scale patterns; (2) we should eliminate triadic chord formations, including not only major and minor chords, but also 7th, 9th, and diminished 7th chords; (3) chord sequences resembling conventional cadences should also be avoided; and (4) the total-chromatic should be used continuously. Serialism itself is normally certain to achieve these objectives. However, we would like to express the view that triads need not be so ruthlessly confiscated. In the right context, at the right moment, they can sound to marvellous effect, and if this suits a composer's aesthetic he should not hesitate to cultivate their occasional use (cf. Example 86).

Later in the section on 'Free twelve-note music' we discussed twelve-note harmony, particularly in connection with two different methods which can be combined into one comprehensive system: (1) conflicting notes, and (2) interval harmony. A fusion of these two methods is imperative for the good harmonic flow of serial music, which thereby can be turned towards a greater degree of atonalism or otherwise, at any moment, as the composer wishes. No other harmonic system seems to exist to control this aspect of serialism.

However, there is one difficulty. Both the use of conflicting notes and that of interval harmony demand freedom in the choice of notes used to control the harmonic flow, and this freedom may be restricted by serialism. But the restriction need not be as great as it first appears. We have already seen how a skilful vertical ordering of parts can turn a brutal set of chords (Example 141) into something much more mellifluous (Example 143), with only the minimal modification of serial principles. The main method used was that of interval harmony, which is adaptable enough to fit in with most serial situations.

There is an alternative. Particularly where the horizontal flow of parts must be good, upper parts can be written first, using serialism. Later a bass can be added to give a good harmonic flow. This bass may be completely free or, if convenient, it may use sections of the series. It should in any case use the total-chromatic consistently.

Naturally, all our comments about the consonant and dissonant qualities of intervals in Chapter 11, 'Interval harmony', apply here also, together with the vital question of the spacing of intervals. The reader is therefore referred back to that section.

Variation forms

These forms abound in serial music, but it is hardly a question of composers varying a theme, as in the old variation technique. It is usually a matter of variations in the use of material, usually of the series itself. In many cases the variations are really a succession of short, separate pieces based on the same series, each piece having a specific character, contrasting with the others, but stylistically unified with them. The result is usually lucid and easy to assimilate.

Some variations are based on a specific formal structure. We have already mentioned the finale of Webern's Symphony Op. 21, with its eleven-bar theme, mirrored at the halfway point, followed in one continuous movement by seven variations and a coda (all mirrored). There is no thematic or other relationship between the theme and any variation — everything changes, except the eleven-bar form. To the innocent listener the form must be imperceptible, and bewildering in its lightning succession of perpetually fugitive events.

Some composers have written extended works on early music (e.g. *The Taverner Fantasy* of Maxwell Davies, Roger Smalley's compendium of pieces based on Blitheman's *Gloria tibi Trinitas*) which are obviously conceived as variation forms. However, any real connection between the old music and the new seems largely ephemeral.

In truth, therefore, serial variation forms have not the theme-based unity of the classical form. They are either based on successions of brief movements, only loosely related, or on the fusion together in one movement of sections based on different musical ideas or constructions. The lucidity or obscurity of the result depends on the composer's aesthetic ideals.

Ostinato forms

In old music some very fine and extended pieces were based on the repetition of an ostinato bass. In modern music we have small ostinato figurations, note-groups or rhythms, which form the background to musical sections. Sometimes they are only brief episodes, or the basis of a variation, but rarely form the foundation of an entire piece. However, one school of composers (using largely diatonic means) has extended ostinato usages to an admirable degree. Using ostinatos in several parts, the components varying gradually, long movements of an emotionally static nature are formed, without complex episodes and retaining a lucid simplicity. There is no reason why the same multiple-ostinato usage could not be adapted to serialism, with the same lucid results.

Contrapuntal forms

We have already discussed these fully in the previous pages, and it remains only for us to point out that contrapuntal forms must be used with an overall formal design in mind. That is, are they to comprise entire movements, to be principal episodes, or to be only very secondary interludes? In truth, continuous polyphony can be hard to digest, and it is well to alternate it with other contrasting episodes which use very different textures. 'Statement and change' is again the rule.

Vocal and choral forms

The span of possibilities here is enormous: we can follow Stravinsky in adapting Medieval forms; we can write songs which are pure melody; or we can use a form which ignores musical values, taking the guise of a word-drama. We have already discussed the possibilities under vocal music, and it would be useless to repeat the arguments. The only thing we would say is that we must have a clear vision of our formal and stylistic intentions before we begin. Even the choice of words must be made with our musical intention in mind, to ensure that they are apt. (I once asked a gifted student to bring me a setting of the *Kyrie*. He returned with a symphonic battle piece, and when I asked if he realized the significance of the words he admitted he did not know what they meant!)

Mirrored structures and palindromes

A palindrome is a musical structure which runs backwards from the halfway point and which therefore reads the same backwards as forwards. It is useful in forming lengthy movements. Sometimes the mirroring may comprise only the note-order, or (conversely) the rhythmic structure set to different notes, so that it is not strictly speaking a palindrome. Sometimes a palindrome is used together with other non-mirrored material and especially in this case the mirroring is not perceived by the listener.

Form in improvisation

Some kinds of improvisation have their form already well defined: jazz improvisation, for example, is based either on a well-known theme or on a familiar harmonic progression (e.g. twelve-bar blues), while the church organist may improvise on a ground bass, a fugal theme, or a chorale melody. In improvisations of a very different kind, a composer may write out different blocks of material, to be played in any order, as the performer wishes. (This is called 'open' form, for the piece can begin and end at any place.)

In improvising, a player can often create spontaneously something much superior to what can be written down with the crude approximation of notation. Indeed, improvisation is a performer's greatest creative act. But he must take care that what he creates builds up to a monolithic whole. We find brilliant improvisers who can create only in bursts of unrelated material, building no overall form, working to no emotive plan. We must not only abide by a precise form, but also build up the right waves of emotion to give it full human significance.

Free form

This term can cover a multitude of sins. In truth, the only real free form is chaos, so we can ignore the adjective 'free' from the start. If we set monkeys to paint a canvas, the result will be 'free' form. If we set a man to paint, he uses an instinctive faculty of 'forming', so that out of chaos something communicative emerges. This creative forming is what we are talking about. In music, chaos is infinitely tiresome. We must form what we do into logically developed emotive communications which hold the listener and then decline. It is strange how all movement in the universe takes the form of waves, from the tiny vibrations within the atom and microscopic organisms to the electric pulses in the brain, the waves of the sea, the throb of sound itself, light waves, radio waves, the pulses of force between galaxies, etc. Musical form is no exception to this natural law.

Music is emotion, and musical forms, however free, must move in waves of emotion. The composer's conception must move forward, hold a peak of tension, and decline into relaxation, ready to begin the next cycle. The length of the cycles can vary, as also the intensity of the peaks. We must plan the emotive path of the whole work so that tranquil periods and emotive peaks find their right places. If we have only rapid successions of frenetic emotive surges, it is obvious that a short piece will result. If we want extended music, we must have long-breathed periods, rather than a rapid rise and decline. (Quick alternations of tension and repose are, of course, possible in this context, but only as episodes, forming part of the larger scheme.)

This wave-form factor is one problem. The other enigma is how to get musical unity between one section of a work and the rest. If there is to be no common musical material we are going to find ourselves with something which, however distinguished, is not distinguishable, and which is therefore of questionable value. The great tragedy of modern music is that, despite an evolution of the musical language to a state of extreme refinement and complexity, the results are less and less significant from a human point of view. The massive resources of IRCAM in creating Boulez's *Répons* produce the latest galaxies of computer-manipulated sounds, which engulf us and bombard us like meteor showers. We soon become impervious to the storm, and afterwards may ask what we have retained. Significantly, my own memory is only of the large wave-forms which made such a maelstrom possible.

13 Indeterminacy, graph scores, text scores, improvisation

Indeterminacy is common in some kinds of contemporary music. It usually entails leaving some aspect of music in an undefined state, to be resolved through the player's own invention. This music is sometimes called 'aleatory' (from the Latin *alea*, a game of dice — hence chance, uncertainty). The parameters which can be indeterminate are usually form, note-duration, speed, pitch, dynamics, tone-colour, and instrumentation. In truth, indeterminacy has existed in music to a small degree for centuries. Many early operas and 'intellectual' music such as Bach's *The Art of Fugue* and parts of *The Musical Offering* had no defined instrumentation, while such factors as speed, dynamics, and tone-colour have long been left to the player's own judgement. However, such parameters as form, note-duration and pitch have long been defined and unalterable. One conspicuous exception has been the 'basso continuo', where a keyboard accompaniment was left to the player's free inventions on a figured bass.

The real objective of modern indeterminacy has been one of clarification and facilitation for both composer and performer. Composers can create indeterminate scores which are simple to play yet which produce a specific effect of some complexity, difficult to notate conventionally. For example, if I want to create an 'interstellar' sound, I need only direct all upper strings to play 'as high as possible', spreading from a single tone to cover a wide cluster, at first playing softly, with occasional fluctuations in volume and pitch. If I need an increase in intensity, each player in turn can change to undulating trills and then a gradual crescendo. Cymbal and tam-tam rolls can be added as intensity grows. At a gesture from the conductor all players can move into the next section (which may be fully notated, or again indeterminate). The shimmering astral effect obtained by this means is quite certain; it can be spread over a reasonable time-span, the score is simple, and rehearsal time need be only a few minutes. To write each part down in full score would mean hours of work, and the sound result would be the same. For the players, too, full notation would create difficulties. Reading music in precise notation would not be easy, with every player's part being different, and rehearsals could drag on boringly. But when each instrumentalist has his own freedom he enjoys creating the music, the performance comes easily, and no time is wasted. The score could be sparingly indicated as shown in Example 144:

Example 144

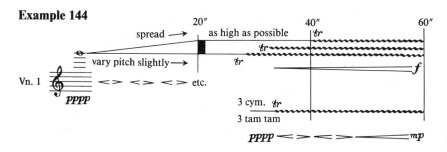

This is a simple illustration, dealing with music of an uncomplicated nature. On the other hand, one can well imagine a situation where several players invent independent, rapid passages based on certain specific designs, which can be improvised in a moment. But to play such passages from notation would require considerable study, and the problems of co-ordination may be acute.

Indeterminacy may be considered a halfway stage to improvisation: players are given definite information on which to work with spontaneous free invention, yet the confines of the music's shape and duration is within bounds determined by the composer. The music therefore benefits from the players' free inventiveness and spontaneity, but the composer maintains the overall definition of the music.

Some composers have deliberately cultivated 'chance' elements in their music. They prefer not to control what succession of events may occur, or what the musical content or design may be. They accept, for better or for worse, whatever happens. This chance element was particularly cultivated by American composers such as Cage, Feldman, and Brown, following the creation of 'open' forms in the plastic arts during the post-war years.

Open forms can be used to create music in which every performance is different. For example, Earle Brown's *Available Forms II* (1962) comprises music for two different orchestral groups, each with its own, independent, conductor. Each group has different music in numbered sections, so devised that each conductor can direct his instrumentalists to play whichever new section he chooses. Every time the piece is played it will therefore have a different form and a different sound-result. This randomness in form need not necessarily lead to music of great diversity, for the method is similar to that of sculptured 'mobiles', which have a number of elements hanging in equilibrium, their relative positions adjustable by the touch of a finger. Overall forms may vary, but the identity of the mobile remains recognizably the same. (Groups of buildings can similarly be seen from different viewpoints, or even from the air, but they can still retain their unity and complete individuality.)

Example 145 shows the work of Haubenstock-Ramati, who specialized in open forms in the 1960s. (Only the top right-hand quarter of the score is shown.) This is a work for six percussionists with a large variety of instruments. The instructions for performance are complex, but from a formal point of view each player begins at a different lettered square and moves horizontally, vertically, or diagonally in any way, changing direction according to certain principles. Notation is either precise or 'proportional' (showing the relative register, volume, and moment-in-time of sounds). Empty fields are silences of varied duration according to the symbols. Total duration is not specified, but the piece ends at a signal from the leader:

Example 145: Haubenstock-Ramati: *Jeux 6*

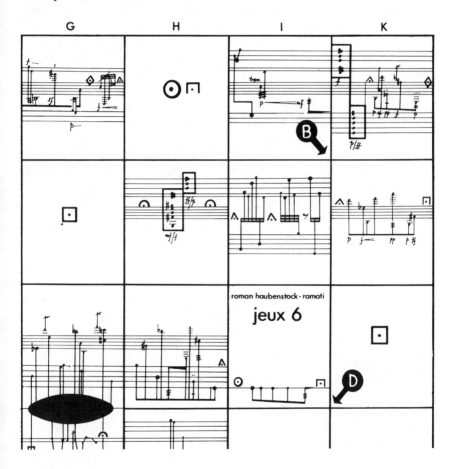

Some composers set out the musical staves in such a way that players are obliged to follow open form alternatives, first taking one route and then another, like a train randomly switching tracks in a shunting yard. Alternatively, the composer may rely on the performer's eye leaping from one musical fragment to another. Example 146 shows part of a page from Sylvano Bussotti's *Siciliano* for twelve male voices. Each singer follows the sequence of fragments he prefers, in any register, at any speed, with the objective of producing music which is 'chaotic and uncontrollable':

Example 146: Bussotti: *Siciliano*

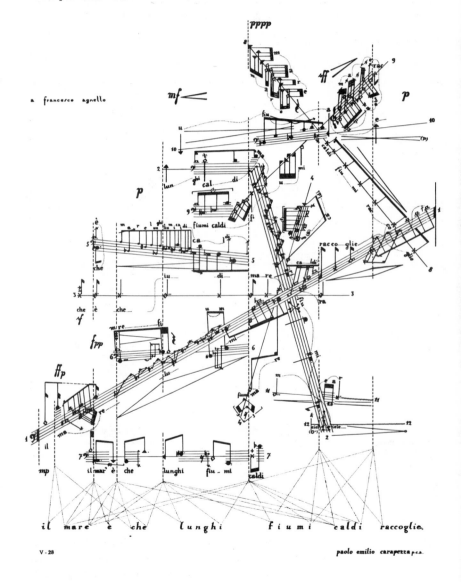

Inevitably, open forms with many free parameters such as the above create an extreme kind of indeterminacy, and if too many performers are involved the result will be chaos, perhaps exciting at first, but ultimately boring. It is therefore preferable to limit indeterminacy to a few parameters within a controlled form.

Indeterminacy in durations has been developed to counter those excessive complexities of involved conventional notation which overburden the player. For example, the following excerpt from *Glose* in Boulez's Third Piano Sonata (another open-form work) seems to have been designed deliberately to baffle the most skilled pianists. This is music without metre or even a sense of 'beat', yet it is notated with extreme precision:

Example 147: Boulez: 'Glose' — Third Piano Sonata

In truth, it was probably Boulez's desire to eliminate 'beat' which led to such complex notation, but other composers have found much simpler solutions, which ease the player's problems enormously. One possibility is to use conventional notation on the understanding that note-values are only approximate suggestions of duration (Example 148):

Example 148: Petrassi: *Nunc,* for guitar

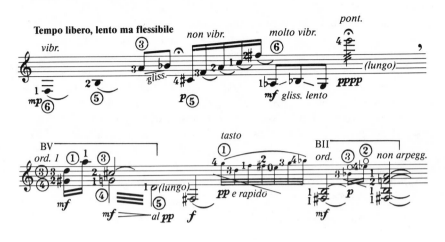

The music must be played freely, and the player must interpret the notation according to his own feelings, with spontaneity. A really creative performance of the above would result in subtle durational values which could hardly be written down, and if they were would prove such an obstacle to the player that most performances would be stilted and lifeless. 'Free' duations therefore aim at encouraging creative, vivid performances. Given this situation, composers sometimes form musical sections which show only pitch successions, leaving performers to create what music they wish:

Example 149: Feldman: *Durations 2*

Here the composer's only instructions are for players to begin together, choose their own durations, and play slowly and smoothly. This score may look naïve and inane, yet it can sound singularly beautiful.

'Boxes' containing note-groups are often used to indicate repetitions of notes, or sometimes notes to be played in any order. Speed and dynamics may be free, and durations varied according to instructions (regular, irregular, etc.). The number of repetitions may be free or may be determined by a given time duration. Example 150 is a singularly successful piece made up of twenty-four boxes, to be played 'as fast as possible' and to have a total duration of two minutes. This means about six repetitions of each box:

Example 150: Brouwer: *la Espiral Eterna*

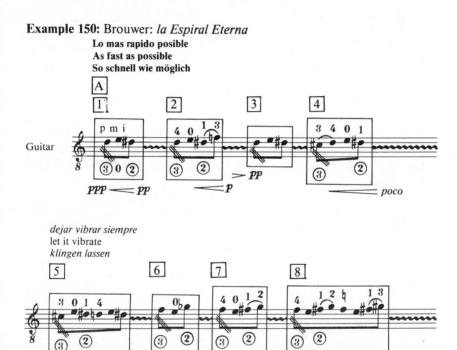

If this piece had been written out in conventional notation, it would have covered six pages of music — tiresome to read, and difficult to play with spontaneity. Instead, the contents of each box can be seen at a glance, easing the player's task enormously; instead of reading hundreds of notes in ordinary notation, he can concentrate on technique and interpretation.

Often, 'proportional' notation is used to suggest the length of sounds, the distance between notes indicating durations. Sometimes this notation is very approximate indeed; sometimes (as in Example 151) it shows all parameters accurately:

Example 151: Bartolozzi: *The Solitary*

In this notation the horizontal lines show note durations, while their thickness indicates volume, crescendos, diminuendos, etc. Fingerings are shown for unusual chordal effects. This type of full notation therefore avoids those complexities which would be created by conventional notation based on beats and metres which do not really exist.

Pitch indeterminacy is used when a composer requires only an approximate contour of notes, to be played freely and perhaps in a given duration. In this way a performer can invent cascades of notes with ease, whereas the same notes in conventional notation would be formidable. A stave is sometimes used, sometimes not. Example 152(a) shows the first and last pitches to be played, all other notes being free as long as they are at the relative height shown. Example 152(b), using staves, is from the string parts of Berio's *Passaggio*, in which rapid designs are outlined. Durations are free, as this example fits in an indeterminate part of the orchestral and choral score:

Example 152a

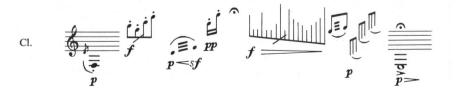

Example 152b: Berio: *Passaggio*

One important factor with pitch indeterminacy is for the player to know whether diatonic or chromatic notes are needed. Clearly, the degree of chromaticism used must suit that written elsewhere in the piece, and the same musical style must be preserved. If this is not already obvious, a descriptive note could avoid gross errors.

Indeterminacy in dynamics has always been common, as past composers have left performers considerable freedom in interpretation. However, in the post-war period of predetermined serialism, dynamic indications became extremely profuse, sometimes being used for every note! (cf. Example 147). However, this excessive usage has been superseded, though more dynamic contrast is usual than previously. But if we leave this parameter indeterminate, players will not use any volume contrast unless we give specific indications. Even then, we may get little. Dynamic contrast is such a vital factor in modern music that if we want it we must make it very evident.

With indeterminacy, it could be said that the composer is abdicating his responsibilities, that the performer is the real creator. This could sometimes well be so. However, I believe that where indeterminacy is used as a helpful means of attaining clearly defined and well-conceived ends, it is perfectly legitimate. It not only provides the composer's desired sound-world, but also restores to players the opportunity for free personal creative expression.

At the risk of restating what should already be obvious, I would stress two things: indeterminacy need not be used for an entire score or movement but can be reserved for small parts or episodes; and, perhaps more important, it can be used at the same time as other material which is completely defined. For example, a fully notated melody may have a background created by indeterminacy, or the 'interstellar' atmosphere created in Example 144 could well be overlaid at intervals by well-defined musical sections. Indeterminacy need not therefore exist in isolation, but can be a valuable addition to fully-composed music.

Graph scores

Composers of the avant-garde school have produced designs, or 'graph scores', of many varied types. Some are accompanied by copious performance instructions which may fill a small volume. Others may provide no instructions at all, the composers preferring a 'chance' performance in which all parameters are free, including the choice of instruments. Whereas the score 'with instructions' may have as its objective a well-defined sound result, that 'without' may be intended only as a stimulus to improvisation, which may follow a course suggested by the design. Example 153 belongs to the latter category:

Example 153: Bussotti: *Piano Piece for David Tudor 3*

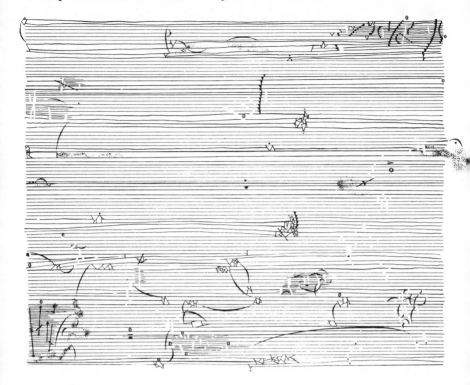

Text scores

Sometimes a musical episode, or even an entire piece, may have no sounds written at all, the composer describing what players should do, or giving indications of mood or mental attitude. Kagel's *Sonant (1960/. . .)* has a volume of instructions, part of it being directions for playing an entire movement without any notation. Players have not only to play but also to recite certain sections, all in timed periods, but without a single sound being printed. This is an extreme case. Other composers may produce a complete score but include brief descriptions here and there to describe what players should do, rather than give them complete notation.

Other text scores aim at inspiring improvisation of a certain kind or creating a psychological attitude. Example 154, from Stockhausen's *Aus den Sieben Tagen* (for ensemble), is typical of the work's sixteen text scores. Obviously the music suggested will be static and slender, so perhaps a text serves the composer's purpose better than a notated score, for he seeks to evoke mood and to subdue or avoid action:

Example 154: Stockhausen: *Aus den Sieben Tagen*

SET SAIL FOR THE SUN

play a tone for so long
until you hear its individual vibrations

hold the tone
and listen to the tones of the others
— to all of them together, not to individual ones —
and slowly move your tone
until you arrive at complete harmony
and the whole sound turns to gold
to pure, gently shimmering fire

Improvisation

Improvisation is involved in much of the music outlined in this chapter. We have already mentioned improvisation forms towards the end of the last chapter, and as we are looking at the subject from the composer's viewpoint, not from the performer's, it remains only for us to make one or two generalizations. Improvisatory elements are very valuable assets in our music, as long as they do not stifle its real identity. They are therefore best used in relatively short, closed sections which have formal precision and are not allowed to overflow in an uncontrolled flood over large, imprecise areas. This is easily arranged if improvisers have to fit in with other instruments playing a set form, a well-defined background, a specific harmonic structure, or a melody (which may be stated or implied).

There is also a question of style. It is important that improvization fits well with our own idiom. In my experience, immature improvisers tend to play in the scale-and-chord idiom of classical music, so if we wish to avoid this we must give some minimal indication of what we prefer. We could give a short passage of the type of music we desire, or a verbal indication such as 'ad lib. chromatic leaps, no scales'. Similarly, a few descriptive words can be more than useful: 'smooth', 'serene', 'harsh', 'rough', 'jagged', 'chaotic', etc. Just a few such descriptive words can work magic, not only from a stylistic viewpoint but also in mood and atmosphere.

14 Practical applications

I should like to make a few brief comments on the practicalities of making 'everyday' music. We may not like it, but it can earn us a living. As musicians we must have many irons in the fire in order to eat. We must seize on whatever chance throws our way, and use it as a stepping stone to better things. (My own career has been very varied. I have done most things, and enjoyed them all, except 'administration'.)

Film and television music

The important thing here is to fall in with the director's ideas. Requirements can differ enormously, and can change with the times. Years ago, films had to have continuous symphonic music from beginning to end. Today, continuous music is used only to hold together poor productions which would fall apart without a constant background noise. Cowboy music may run right through a movie about mid-West urban nightlife. South American music may knit together brief snippets of a documentary on Nicaraguan guerilla warfare. Music of any kind helps create continuity, as long as it is not wildly unsuitable.

On a more artistic plane, there are several alternatives:
Films without music. Many good films need only natural sounds to supplement the vision (e.g. the wash of the sea, bird-song, traffic noise, etc.). All films must have some kind of sound, even if it is only the sound of 'silence'; a dead sound track gives a poor sense of reality.

Films with only title music. Music supports the titles, giving interest to what can be a boring period. Similarly, the film ends best with music behind the final titles and credits. In any case, music serves to give a true sense of 'beginning' and 'ending'. Nothing can do it better.

Theme music. This is similar to films with only title music, but here the music is more than a back-up. Many television series or programmes begin with special theme music which is always the same, strongly identifying the programme. For example, theme music is used for news programmes, football matches and horse-jumping competitions, as well as for long series about the Pallisers or the intrigues of Texas oil tycoons.

Actuality music. Sometimes an actual musical performance is filmed. We may hear a pop singer, a pianist, or native drummers. This calls for a very real sensation of performance through good synchronization and realistic sound and acoustics.

Mood music. This is the real art of film or television music, where sound not only intensifies the atmosphere of the vision, but also introduces a specific emotional undertone which prepares us to meet the coming dramatic situation. For instance, the same country scene can be made, through music, the setting for human situations which are happy or sad, serene, sinister, or tragic. This kind of mood music need only be introduced occasionally, in a film which otherwise has only natural sound.

It is best to introduce mood music in such a way that its beginning goes unnoticed. In fact, if film music does its work properly it will not be consciously 'heard'. If it is too obvious it will distract attention from the action.

One of the most subtle functions of mood music is to prepare us, almost subconsciously, for new action or a change of mood which would otherwise be too sudden or crude (and without music would need long dramatic preparation). For example, we may see a peaceful scene, the heroine quietly reading, and gradually be made aware, through the music, that something sinister is going to happen. It tells us exactly when the doorhandle is going to turn, and we are ready for a fright. How could it be done otherwise? The reverse can also happen — music can lead us from violence and chaos into peace and serenity, without even a change of scene.

Mood music is therefore best reserved for periods of general emotional intensification (scenes of romance, conflict, stress, etc.) or for those subtle atmosphere changes we have just described. Elsewhere, natural sound is preferable, as continuous music is tiresome. It can also confuse speech![1]

Descriptive music was once used synchronized with movement, such as a ball bouncing downstairs, a man slipping on a banana skin. But this kind of usage is now rare except in cartoons.

Naturally, title music should be a suitable preparation for what is to follow. It should set the emotive tone and prepare us for the historical period. Before the vision starts, a Vivaldian score prepares us for an 18th-century country-house drama, while some raucous hot jazz will say 'this is city life in America in the 1920s'. Title music is often quite brief — no more than two minutes —

[1] Speech can be confused particularly by prominent sounds in the same pitch zone.

and it may have to change considerably during its course. It may have to be strident for a title such as *The Siege of Tobruk*, but by the time the vision begins it may be required to emanate a still expectancy, as we see a desert dawn, the sand blowing over the debris of battle.

Theme music, on the other hand, used repeatedly for many productions in series, may not have the element of change just described. It is often a precise piece fitting the exact duration of titles and credits which begin and end each production. In this case, theme music will suit the series in general and ignore the mood which is to follow.

Instrumentation must suit the subject. A historical tale should have music to suit its period, so we may need several instrumental groups (and acoustics) to suit various situations − e.g. brass fanfares in the open air, monks' voices in the cathedral, lutes and viols in the king's court. A science fiction subject can have electronic music alone. 'Classical' groups, such as the string quartet and piano trio, should be avoided because of concert hall associations. The worst instrumentation I have heard was the use of Bach's organ chorale preludes in the Italian film *The Tree of the Wooden Clogs*. The atmosphere of gloom suited this sad tale of peasants in the Po valley, but the sound of the organ was quite wrong.

We must avoid musical forms which do not suit situations. I have heard car chases accompanied by fugues which may be busy and exciting but aesthetically are ridiculously unsuited to the action. However, I must admit that the general public does not notice what is obvious to a musician. I once took my sister-in-law to see an Italian film about a cancer operation. The music made me so ill I had to leave the cinema. When I explained to her that the music had made me ill, she said 'what music'? This confirms what I said before − good film music is not even noticed (except perhaps by musicians).

Speed is essential. You can be sure that at a certain point the director will want the music 'yesterday'. Get to know the script and locations as soon as possible, and prepare suitable material. Title music can be written at an early stage, and this can often form the basis of what follows. At a certain point the footage of film will become available, or the television script will be issued with timings of all scenes and speech. The durations of all musical sections can now be decided, together with exact points where emotional changes will be needed. Bearing in mind that everything may be altered the next day, the music can be sketched out. Leave the orchestration till the end, because it is a sad waste of time to have to scrap complete scores.

New music is not needed for every situation. Good film writers use only a little material, skilfully adapted to every scene and emotion. One famous series of thriller films has music formed from a simple succession of three chords and a melodic fragment. This material is manipulated in a thousand ways, but nobody has said it is 'monotonous'. Probably, they have never noticed it. Alternatively, the title music can be adapted for all other needs.

Such economy is essential for speed. In a trade where time is of the essence, we cannot afford the luxury of waiting for inspiration.

Where timing is so critical, music must be recorded either with a stopwatch or while the film is projected. And because time is money, no mistakes can be made. Fortunately we can now use tape editing, so there is no need for the precision which existed before the advent of tape in 1950. However, I find it useful to have 'elastic' parts of the score which can be stretched out or cut off. For example, repeating parts can be cut out, or sustained chords can be faded out or held on as necessary.

As economy is vital, begin a recording session with all the players, then reduce ensemble groups until only the solo guitarist is left. Thus the risk of overtime costs can be kept to a minimum. Unfortunately, this means that the music is not in its proper sequence. Always stay on to put everything in the right order. Don't believe a technician who says he can do it himself (I once did, and the film was issued with music in the wrong order throughout!).

I think we can learn most from other people's films and mistakes. Make a habit of critical listening and analysing. And remember, it will only be after a superb film score that you will realize you never heard a note!

Jazz

Though the word 'jazz' is now used for popular dance music earlier in this century, its basic principles are still used in many kinds of popular music. It is largely musical style and idiom which can turn a melody into one form or another. For example, some themes from Bizet's *Carmen* have been restyled as jazz, South American sambas, rock, or pop songs simply by a change of setting and a 'twist' to the melody. So though I may be writing about jazz, I am really outlining other possibilities too.

Jazz is usually based on three principal factors: a distinctive melody; a precise form; and well-defined harmonic progressions. In many pieces the words may come first. A 'lyric' writer may work with a melody-writer or invent the tune himself, but the original idea is often the lyrics. However, strongly individual melodic lines are essential, and for the sake of memorability, there will probably be a good deal of repetition — in fact many phrases may be almost identical:

Example 155: Thomas 'Fats' Waller: *Honeysuckle Rose*

Notice how each rhythmic shape is very similar, and based on a precise length. The form of jazz pieces often allows for a period of melodic contrast after the first phrases have been well established. For instance, the eight bars of Example 155 form the A section of a thirty-two-bar piece based on the form AABA, in which B has a melody of contrasting contour and rhythm together with different harmony. This form is very usual in jazz pieces, the B portion often being in a related key and modulating back to the tonic for the last A section.

However, some pieces omit a contrasting B section, in which case three statements of A create a twenty-four-bar scheme, or two statements only sixteen bars.

The twelve-bar blues form is also very well defined, usually comprising three similar melodic phrases of four bars each, the harmonic scheme normally following the pattern:

bars: 1   2   3   4   5   6   7   8   9   10   11   12
|C |F |C |C7 |F——|—— |C——|—— |G7——|—— |C F |C |

This harmonic pattern gives the 'blues' character, and is fairly standardized. But other jazz pieces have very diverse harmonic schemes. Though formulas such as C–A minor–D Minor–G7–C are common enough, the best jazz writers usually aimed at distinctive harmonies. Some had a genius for beautiful harmony of an inevitable quality, which could hardly be bettered (Example 156):

Example 156: Hoagy Carmichael: *Stardust*

This sample of Hoagy Carmichael shows melody of outstanding quality in a harmonic setting which few great composers could improve on. Though the piano part is fully written out, it may be considerably altered by players who prefer to elaborate their own accompaniments from chord symbols.

We have deliberately delayed mentioning that many songs were of the 'verse and chorus' type — in other words, a special 'verse' introduction will precede the chorus or 'refrain'. This is also typical of popular songs today, but as the verse section is less important, and is often omitted, we have preferred to delay discussion till now. All we need say is that the form of the verse section is very variable as it depends on the words. It can be either quite short or long, but as it is introductory material the music is less important than the refrain and is seldom as distinguished.

Pop songs

There have been many streams of jazz since the 1950s, but these developments are outside our study. However, as 'pop' is quite distinct, we can usefully comment on its characteristics.

Pop can be very similar to jazz, but in its most characteristic form it seems to be a simplification of jazz, the main technical and stylistic factors being reduced to elementary formulas. Melody is largely repetitive, with square two- or four-bar phrases. Contrasting sections of substance may be avoided, and the same basic thematic phrase may be repeated with little change for a large part of the piece. The forms are less precise than jazz forms, where the formal outlines are well defined by theme and harmony. With the repetitive phrases of pop the sense is one of continuity, without gravitation towards an ending. This rather static thematic situation is reinforced by the harmonic position. Here, change is largely avoided, especially change which uses striking harmonies. Harmony is elementary through force of circumstance, as it must suit the static thematic and formal position. However, the above describes pop in its most extreme state. In less extreme situations, it can include many of the more evolved characteristics of jazz, making for hybrid pieces which belong to both worlds.

In pop songs, the words are often the most striking feature. One could say they make the song, for they are often more distinguished than the music. They too are often repetitive, and rarely tell a story or paint a large canvas. They are not meant to, for a static quality is preferred.

The most prominent feature of pop is the 'beat'. This is usually strongly accentuated, with a forceful rhythm section producing a large noise element. In many recordings this accompaniment is so powerful that the theme can hardly be heard. This would seem to indicate that 'beat' is more important than any other factor except possibly the words.

Many performances of pop begin with the gradual formation of the accompaniment pattern. Once this is established, the song or theme can begin. This may be presented in various ways (e.g. first sung softly, then instrumental solo, then sung loudly with choral backing, etc.), and then at the end the music is faded out. This is because the theme does not arrive at a strongly defined conclusion, nor is a sense of finality desired. In order to get more extended performances, pop sometimes uses a technical trick which gives a moment of uplift and interest. At the beginning of a thematic repetition, the tonality of the refrain is suddenly lifted a semitone. This is sometimes done two or three times to create a longer performance and to build a crescendo of interest in the final sections.

Pop resembles black music in many ways — the forceful beat, repetitive words and melody, simple harmony, formal continuity, repetition creating static moods, etc. The means are more sophisticated (especially if one considers pop's armoury of amplified instruments), but the musical essentials are the same.

Longer compositions

I am well aware that this book has not dwelt on how to write string quartets and symphonies. One could (with a small grain of truth) say that long works are only extensions of shorter compositions, and that we need only to stretch our ideas over bigger areas. But this would not really be true. The truth is that the ability to write extended works is born of mature mental attitudes and technical skills. This is quite beyond the capabilities of beginners, and for them to write long works without first being competent in short ones would be to court disaster. Therefore, I believe it essential for readers to become skilled in short works based on the ideas presented here, gradually maturing their techniques and forming personal styles and idioms, before undertaking the weighty task of longer works. It is much better to fill our waste baskets with dozens of short experiments of investigation than with rejected pages of quartets and symphonies, which may well have cost us much in blood and sweat, without teaching us more than we already know.

My recommendation is therefore deliberately to avoid undertaking longer works until the contents of this book have been assimilated and the reading well supplemented by studies of major scores from a historical and analytical viewpoint. Composers have always 'stood on each other's shoulders', and by learning from our predecessors we are only following a well-tried custom.

Exercises

The following questions must be regarded as only samples of the work needed to cover the wide range of material discussed in this book. It is left to students and teachers to increase the number of exercises in their own particular spheres of interest. Nevertheless, though the number of exercises has been deliberately limited, they are designed to be widely varied and comprise a broad field of studies.

Chapter 4: Melody (pages 13–34)

(1) The following are the rhythmic patterns of the first phrases of three well-known melodies. Choose your own pitch-successions to form your own themes.

(2) The following are the pitch-successions of the first phrases of three well-known themes. Choosing your own rhythmic designs, use these notes to create the beginnings of your own melodies.

(3) Use the rhythmic cell ♩ ♪♫ and its reversal to form the first phrase of a melody. (cf. Elgar's *Enigma Variations* in Example 12)

(4) Use the three cells ♪♫ , ♫♪ , ♫ to form a melody. The cells can be used in varied orders, and also abbreviated or expanded. (Example 14)

(5) Use the following theme as a basis for decorated melody in the baroque style, as in Example 15.

Ob.

(6) Begin a 'melody by growth' for flute using the 4-note nucleus B, A♯, G, and C♯, following Messiaen's example in Example 16.

(7) Continue the following melody based on non-repetition, following the style of the sample given:

Cl.

(8) Complete any of the above melodies, paying particular attention to the creation of convincing overall form, and the choice of forms suitable to the melodic material.

Chapter 5: Harmony and counterpoint (pages 35–48)

Harmony

(1) Harmonize the following chorale melody in four parts. Treat this as an exercise in avoiding root positions (except for the last chord), so that there is ample variety in the kind of inversion used, and in the role of the bass.

(2) Write a short passacaglia for organ, using the following ground bass and changing the role of the bass in the repetitions so that it functions in many ways, and produces varied harmonies.

(3) Use the following as the melody in a String Trio. Keep the other parts as simple as you wish, but treat the exercise as an experiment in *minimal* harmonic change. There may therefore be many melody notes which do not belong to the harmony.

(4) Write an organ prelude beginning as follows, using the bass indicated. The harmony used must be *chromatic harmony*.

Counterpoint

(1) Continue the following as a short movement based on *canon at the octave*:

2 Vni.

(2) Write a piece for organ using *canon by inversion*, beginning as follows:

Organ

(3) Write a *canon by augmentation* based on the following, in which the lower part has twice the note-values of the upper part. The second half of the upper part must bear a logical relationship to the first half.

Pfte.

(4) Write a *canon cancrizans* for two violins beginning as follows. (The ending will be a reversal of these parts.)

Vn. 1

Vn. 2

Chapter 6: Vocal writing (pages 49–58)

(1) Set the following words as a strophic song, using the same music for some verses, while treating other verses differently, creating a convincing overall form which has both diversity and constancy.

'Beautie, Truth, and Raritie,
Grace in all simplicitie,
Here enclosde, in cinders lie.

Death is now the *Phoenix* nest,
And the *Turtles* loyall brest,
To eternitie doth rest.

Leaving no posteritie,
Twas not their infirmitie,
It was married Chastitie.

Truth may seeme, but cannot be,
Beautie bragge, but tis not she,
Truth and Beautie buried be.

To this urne let those repaire,
That are either true or faire,
For these dead Birds, sigh a prayer.'

(From *The Phoenix and Turtle* by Shakespeare)

(2) Abbreviate the following poem by at least 50% in order to make it more suitable for a musical setting. Naturally, the full meaning and style must be retained.

'Faire as unshaded Light, or as the Day
In its first birth, when all the Year was May;
Sweet as the Altars smoke, or as the new
Unfolded Bud, swell'd by the early dew;
Smooth, as the face of waters first appear'd,
Ere Tides began to strive, or Winds were heard:
Kind as the willing Saints, and calmer farre,
Than in their sleeps forgiven Hermits are:
You that are more, than our discreeter feare
Dares praise, with such full Art, what make you here?
Here where the summer is so little seen,
That leaves (her cheapest wealth) scarce reach at green,
You come, as if the silver planet were

Misled a while from her much injur'd Sphere,
And t'ease the travailes of her beames to night,
In this small Lanthorn would contract her light.'

(*To the Queen, entertain'd at night
by the Countess of Anglesey* by D'Avenant)

(3) Set your abbreviation of the above poem to melody.

(4) Write non-strophic melody for the following words. The style must be strongly lyrical and may be non-metrical.

'Grief has grown
Among the fragments
Of the days.
It has settled,
Found footing,
And climbed
As a vine
About the rocks.
The roots are deep,
And the vines are strong.'

(From *Variation in Verse* by John Gracen Brown)[1]

Chapters 7 & 8: Introductions, accompaniments, and orchestration
(pages 59–74)

(1) Write introductions and accompaniments for the exercises written for Chapter 6, using the piano only. (It is more fruitful to experiment with a wide variety of material for the beginnings of the songs, rather than concentrate on making complete works at first.)
(2) Write piano introductions and the first bars of accompaniments designed to support songs of different emotive moods: placid, funereal, confident, sad, joyous, vigorous, etc.
(3) Orchestrate the introductions and accompaniments written for the previous questions.

---

[1] 'Grief has Grown' from *Variation in Verse* by John Gracen Brown has been reprinted courtesy of Branden Press, Inc. 21 Station Street, Brookline Village, MA 02147.

Chapter 9: Choral music (pages 75–87)

(1) Use the following words to experiment with different choral textures such as homophony with and without independent movement, monophony, pairing, solo and accompaniment, layering, multiple parts, etc.

'With my face turned to the orient
to await the dawn,
With my heart turned to a brighter orient
from which will come the resurrection,

I lay me down. What matter
if it be for one night or for all?
My Lord guides me
towards the dawn and the resurrection!'

(*Notturno* by Margherita Guidacci)[1]

(2) Set the following words for choir using Renaissance-type note patterns, but produce a 'modern' effect by obscuring the harmony evenly.

'Puer natus in Bethlehem, alleluia:
Unde gaudet Jerusalem, alleluia, alleluia.
In cordis jubilo Christum natum adoremus,
Cum novo cantico. Alleluia.'

Chapter 10: Technical expansions 1: (pages 88–110)

Free pentatonic music

(1) Continue the harmonization of the following *Kyrie*, using only notes of the pentatonic mode D, E, G, A, and B. The harmonic characteristics must be largely maintained (i.e. contrary motion between outer parts, avoidance of conventional triad chords, etc.).

Choir

Ky - ri - e____ e - le - i - son._____

etc.

---

[1] From *Paglia e Polvere* by Margherita Guidacci, published by Rebellato, Cittadella Veneta.

Chri - - ste e - le - i - son.

Ky - ri - e e - - le i - son.

Free diatonicism

(1) Continue the following piano piece, using a free diatonic language similar to that indicated:

Pfte.

mf etc.

(2) Continue the following for five-part brass ensemble in the idiom indicated. Use free diatonicism, avoiding conventional triad chords to a large extent.

Allegro

3 Tr.

f etc.

2 Tbni.

The whole-tone scale

(1) Continue the following clarinet melody using the whole-tone idiom:

Andante

Cl.

mp etc.

(2) Continue the following piano piece, using the whole-tone technique. Keep to the same scale throughout.

Pfte.

etc.

Bitonality and polytonality

(1) Continue the following duo for flute and clarinet, using a bitonal scheme in E minor and G minor. Though the exercise begins in canon, there is no need to keep rigidly to canonic devices throughout.

Fl.

Cl.

(2) Continue the following using a polytonal scheme of G major (flute), B flat major (oboe) and E major (bassoon):

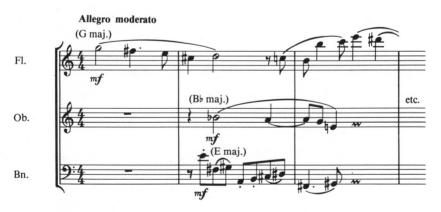

Fl.

Ob.

Bn.

(3) Continue the following using a bitonal scheme in the upper parts and a freely chromatic bass in the lower part:

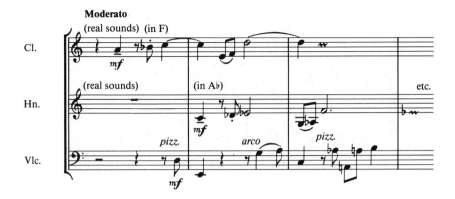

Harmony in fourths

(1) Using a single series of fourths (comprising the total-chromatic), begin a piano piece as follows. Transpose the series for the central portion of the piece and then return to the original series.

(2) Complete the following *Agnus Dei*. Use only the notes D, G, C, and F in various registers for the first line. For the second, move into transposed fourth groups, and return to the original group for the last section. The words are as follows:

Agnus Dei, qui tollis peccata mundi, miserere nobis.
Agnus Dei, qui tollis peccata mundi, miserere nobis.
Agnus Dei, qui tollis peccata mundi, dona nobis pacem.

(3) Continue the following organ piece based on perfect and augmented fourths in various transpositions:

Chapter 11: Technical expansions 2: (pages 111–24)

Substitution notes

(1) Complete a short organ prelude in chromatic harmony, with prominent use of substitution notes, using the bass indicated:

Conflicting notes

(1) *a* Add conflicting notes to the following consonant note-groups in order to produce an even flow of dissonant chords in 3 parts.
b Add a further bass in order to produce a good harmonic flow featuring a moderate degree of dissonance in 4-part chords.

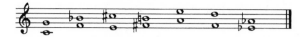

Interval harmony

(1) *a* Add a third part to the dissonant note-groups below in order to create more consonant harmony.

b Add a bass to the above as a fourth part which will create a good harmonic flow.

(2) Add a free part below the following haphazard succession of consonant and dissonant intervals in order to create chordal progressions which are (a) of relatively uniform mild tension, (b) of uniformly strong tension, (c) at first consonant, then progressing towards maximum dissonance about mid-way, and then gradually returning to consonance:

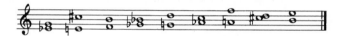

(3) Add a fourth part as a bass below, or a treble above, the three-part chords created in the previous question in order to form good twelve-note harmony of even tension throughout.

Free twelve-note music

(1) Continue the following piano movement using the free twelve-note technique:

(2) Complete the following trio for two violins and cello in a free twelve-note style, retaining the semi-canonic manner of composition:

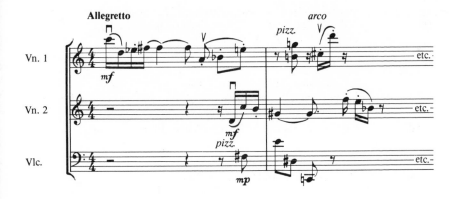

Chapter 12: Serialism (pages 125–47)

Various kinds of Series and their Derived Forms

(1) Beginning with the notes A, B♭, and E, continue with nine different notes to produce (a) tonal, (b) atonal, and (c) symmetrical series.

(2) Write the derived forms of the three series in the previous question.

Writing melody

(1) Below are the beginnings of two melodies. Complete the series and write violin melodies of 'traditional' types, with phrase repetitions and constructions using the rhythmic material given.

(2) Complete the series and continue the following melody for flute, about 16 bars in all. The melody must be of a lyrical nature, though less 'traditional' than those in Question 1. Note-groups and rhythmic shapes may be repeated. Intensify the thematic material around bar 11 and then end with tranquility.

(3) Write a clarinet solo in a vigorous style. Do not repeat any rhythms or note-groups. Use irregular phrases and jagged phrase outlines, while exploiting the differently-coloured registers of the instrument.

Accompaniments

(1) Write various kinds of accompaniment for the above melodies, i.e. simple harmonization; imitations of thematic material; special motifs and rhythmic figurations, etc. It is sufficient to establish the accompaniment patterns for only a few bars, then use the same material to create introductions before the melody begins.

Polyphonic writing

(1) Using the series indicated, continue the following *Canon at the octave* for two clarinets for about 16 bars:

(2) Write a *canon by inversion* in two parts, for flute and cello, using 'O' and 'I' versions of the series used in Question 1:

(3) Write a short piece for two horns using *canon cancrizans* form. (The upper part will end with a retrograde of the lower one, and *vice versa*.)

(4) Continue the following as a *rhythmic canon* for clarinet and bassoon, using the series indicated by the succession of 12 notes:

The horizontal-vertical method

(1) Continue the following piano piece in the form of melody and accompaniment, all parts sharing the same series (and its derived forms) as indicated:

Chapter 14: Practical applications (pages 160–7)

Film and TV music

(1) Write a few bars of 'title music', and then use the same material to create different atmospheres: peace, excitement, waiting, suspense, speed in movement, etc.

(2) Write a complete score for the beginning of a TV documentary designed to condemn blood sports. Use only a small, economical ensemble, choosing the most effective instruments. The duration of the score is only 1′30″, and there is no dialogue. The visual sequence is as follows:

0′0″	English countryside, misty.
0′10″	Woodland.
0′15″	Close-up of fox cub.
0′25″	Countryside as before. Hunting pack in distance.
0′35″	Fox mother in movement.
0′50″	Return to fox cub.
1′05″	Countryside. Pack closer.
1′15″	Fox mother moving into distance.
1′20″	Pack following.
1′25″	Pack disappearing in distance.
1′30″	Music fades behind voice commentary.

(Note: the timings suggest fragmentation, but the music should create continuity rather than change.)

Jazz and pop songs

(1) Using the 12-bar blues sequence of harmonies, write a melody in blues style.

(2) Continue the following as a pop song, including harmony symbols and suggestions for a bass line:

Index